Modern Critical Interpretations

George Eliot's
Middlemarch

Modern Critical Interpretations

These and other titles in preparation

Modern Critical Interpretations

George Eliot's
Middlemarch

Edited and with an introduction by
Harold Bloom
Sterling Professor of the Humanities
Yale University

Chelsea House Publishers ◊ *1987*
NEW YORK ◊ NEW HAVEN ◊ PHILADELPHIA

Library of Congress Cataloging-in-Publication Data

George Eliot's Middlemarch.
    (Modern critical interpretations)
    Bibliography: p.
    Includes index.
    1. Eliot, George, 1819–1880. Middlemarch.
I. Bloom, Harold.   II. Series.
PR4662.G4   1987   823'.8   86-34300
ISBN 0-87754-739-4 (alk. paper)

Contents

Editor's Note

This book gathers together a representative selection of the best modern criticism of George Eliot's strongest novel, *Middlemarch*. The critical essays are reprinted here in the chronological order of their original publication. I am grateful to Cornelia Pearsall for her aid in editing this volume.

My introduction centers upon George Eliot as a prophet of the Moral Sublime, and upon Dorothea Brooke as a heroine of the Protestant Will. J. Hillis Miller, most genial and helpful of deconstructors, begins the chronological sequence of criticism with his essay upon the relation between George Eliot's mode of vision and her "insight into the dismaying dangers of metaphor." In Barbara Hardy's exegesis of the relation between public and private worlds in *Middlemarch*, the book is acclaimed as "the most remarkable example before *Ulysses* of a novel about past and present."

Kathleen Blake argues that *Middlemarch* is a great feminist work, a judgment with which I believe George Eliot herself would have disagreed. In a notable deconstruction, Neil Hertz explores some of Eliot's deepest negative insights, some of them centering upon her most famous passage that attains a Sublime apotheosis in: "and we should die of that roar which lies on the other side of silence."

Jan B. Gordon examines *Middlemarch* as a dialectic of origins and endings, in which the fictive world's center moves from self-consciousness to the image of the child, unconscious and unhistoric. A Dantean model for figures of knowledge in the novel is posited by Alexander Welsh, as he pursues the figurative scheme of blackmail in George Eliot. In this book's final essay, Patricia McKee concentrates upon the prelude to *Middlemarch*, finding there George Eliot's refusal as narrator to impose a single idea of order that could take the place of knowledge. Instead, Eliot's narrative project is seen as one that embraces multiple alternatives of meaning, many prospective ideas of order.

Introduction

I

*Even taken in its derivative meaning of outline, what is form but the limit of
that difference by which we discriminate one object from another?—a limit
determined partly by the intrinsic relations or composition of the object, &
partly by the extrinsic action of other bodies upon it. This is true whether
the object is a rock or a man.*

GEORGE ELIOT, "Notes on Forms in Art"

It was Freud, in our time, who taught us again what the pre-Socratics
taught: *ethos* is the *daimon*, character is fate. A generation before Freud,
George Eliot taught the same unhappy truth to her contemporaries. If
character is fate, then in a harsh sense there can be no accidents. Character
presumably is less volatile than personality, and we tend to disdain anyone
who would say: personality is fate. Personalities suffer accidents; characters endure fate. If we seek major personalities among the great novelists,
we find many competitors: Balzac, Tolstoi, Dickens, Henry James, even
the enigmatic Conrad. By general agreement, the grand instance of a
moral character would be George Eliot. She has a nearly unique spiritual
authority, best characterized by the English critic Walter Allen about
twenty years ago:

> George Eliot is the first novelist in the world in some things,
> and they are the things that come within the scope of her moral
> interpretation of life. Circumscribed though it was, it was cer-
> tainly not narrow; nor did she ever forget the difficulty atten-
> dant upon the moral life and the complexity that goes to its
> making.

Her peculiar gift, almost unique despite her place in a tradition of displaced Protestantism that includes Samuel Richardson's *Clarissa* and

1

Wordsworth's poetry, is to dramatize her interpretations in such a way as to abolish the demarcations between aesthetic pleasure and moral renunciation. Richardson's heroine, Clarissa Harlowe, and Wordsworth in his best poems share in a compensatory formula: experiential loss can be transformed into imaginative gain. Eliot's imagination, despite its Wordsworthian antecedents, and despite the ways in which Clarissa Harlowe is the authentic precursor of Dorothea Brooke in *Middlemarch,* is too severe to accept the formula of compensation. The beauty of renunciation in Eliot's fiction does not result from a transformation of loss, but rather from a strength that is in no way dependent upon exchange or gain. Eliot presents us with the puzzle of what might be called the Moral Sublime. To her contemporaries, this was no puzzle. F. W. H. Myers, remembered now as a "psychic researcher" (a marvelous metaphor that we oddly use as a title for those who quest after spooks) and as the father of L. H. Myers, author of the novel *The Near and the Far,* wrote a famous description of Eliot's 1873 visit to Cambridge:

> I remember how at Cambridge I walked with her once in the Fellows' Garden of Trinity, on an evening of rainy May; and she, stirred somewhat beyond her wont, and taking as her text the three words which had been used so often as the inspiring trumpet-call of men—the words God, Immortality, Duty—pronounced with terrible earnestness how inconceivable was the first, how unbelievable was the second, and yet how peremptory and absolute the third. Never, perhaps, have sterner accents confirmed the sovereignty of impersonal and unrecompensing Law. I listened, and night fell; her grave, majestic countenance turned towards me like a sybil's in the gloom; it was as though she withdrew from my grasp, one by one, the two scrolls of promise and left me the third scroll only, awful with inevitable fates. And when we stood at length and parted, amid that columnar circuit of forest trees, beneath the last twilight of starless skies, I seemed to be gazing, like Titus at Jerusalem, on vacant seats and empty halls—on a sanctuary with no Presence to hallow it, and heaven left empty of God.

However this may sound now, Myers intended no ironies. As the sybil of "unrecompensing Law," Eliot joined the austere company of nineteenth-century prose prophets: Carlyle, Ruskin, Newman, and Arnold in England; Emerson in America; Schopenhauer, Nietzsche, Kierkegaard, and finally Freud on the Continent. But this ninefold, though storytellers of a sort, wrote no novels. Eliot's deepest affinities were scarcely with Dickens, Thackeray, and Trollope, and yet her formal achievement requires us to read her as we read them. This causes difficulties, since Eliot was not a great stylist, and was far more immersed in philosophical than in narrative tradition. Yet her frequent clumsiness in authorial asides and her hesitations in storytelling matter not at all. We do not even regret her absolute lack of any sense of the comic, which never dares take revenge upon her anyway. Wordsworth at his strongest, as in "Resolution and Independence," still can be unintentionally funny (which inspired the splendid parodies of the poem's leech-gatherer and its solipsistic bard in Lewis Carroll's "White Knight's Ballad," and Edward Lear's "Incidents in the Life of My Uncle Arly"). But I have seen no effective parodies of George Eliot, and doubt their possibility. It is usually unwise to be witty concerning our desperate need, not only to decide upon right action, but also to will such action, against pleasure and against what we take to be self-interest. Like Freud, Eliot ultimately is an inescapable moralist, precisely delineating our discomfort with culture, and remorselessly weighing the economics of the psyche's civil wars.

II

George Eliot is not one of the great letter writers. Her letters matter because they are hers, and in some sense do tell part of her own story, but they do not yield to a continuous reading. On a scale of nineteenth-century letter-writing by important literary figures, in which Keats would rank first, and Walter Pater last (the Paterian prose style is never present in his letters), Eliot would find a place about dead center. She is always herself in her letters, too much herself perhaps, but that self is rugged, honest, and formidably inspiring. Our contemporary feminist critics seem to me a touch uncomfortable with Eliot. Here she is on extending the franchise to women, in a letter to John Morley (May 14, 1867):

> Thanks for your kind practical remembrance. Your attitude in relation to Female Enfranchisement seems to be very nearly mine. If I were called on to act in the matter, I would certainly not oppose any plan which held out a reasonable promise of tending to establish as far as possible an equivalence of advantages for the two sexes, as to education and the possibilities of free development. I fear you may have misunderstood something I said the other evening about nature. I never meant to urge the "intention of Nature" argument, which is to me a piti-

able fallacy. I mean that as a fact of mere zoological evolution, woman seems to me to have the worst share in existence. But for that very reason I would the more contend that in the moral evolution we have "an art which does mend nature"—an art which "itself is nature." It is the function of love in the largest sense, to mitigate the harshness of all fatalities. And in the thorough recognition of that worse share, I think there is a basis for a sublimer resignation in woman and a more regenerating tenderness in man.

However, I repeat that I do not trust very confidently to my own impressions on this subject. The peculiarities of my own lot may have caused me to have idiosyncrasies rather than an average judgment. The one conviction on the matter which I hold with some tenacity is, that through all transitions the goal towards which we are proceeding is a more clearly discerned distinctness of function (allowing always for exceptional cases of individual organization) with as near an approach to equivalence of good for woman and for man as can be secured by the effort of growing moral force to lighten the pressure of hard non-moral outward conditions. It is rather superfluous, perhaps injudicious, to plunge into such deeps as these in a hasty note, but it is difficult to resist the desire to botch imperfect talk with a little imperfect writing.

This is a strong insistence upon form in life as in art, upon the limit of that difference by which we discriminate one object from another. I have heard feminist critics decry it as defeatism, though Eliot speaks of "mere zoological evolution" as bringing about every woman's "worse share in existence." "A sublimer resignation in woman" is not exactly a popular goal these days, but Eliot never speaks of the Sublime without profundity and an awareness of human loss. When she praises Ruskin as a teacher "with the inspiration of a Hebrew prophet," she also judges him to be "strongly akin to the sublimest part of Wordsworth," a judgment clearly based upon the Wordsworthian source of Ruskin's tropes for the sense of loss that dominates the Sublime experience. The harshness of being a woman, however mitigated by societal reform, will remain, Eliot reminds us, since we cannot mend nature and its unfairness. Her allusion to the Shakespearean "art which does mend nature," and which "itself is nature" (*Winter's Tale*, 1 4.4.88–96) subtly emends Shakespeare in the deliberately wistful hope for a moral evolution of love between the sexes. What dominates this letter to Morley is a harsh plangency, yet it is anything but defeatism. Perhaps Eliot should have spoken of a "resigned sublimity" rather than a "sublime resignation," but her art, and life, give the lie to any contemporary feminist demeaning of the author of *Middlemarch*, who shares with Jane Austen and Emily Dickinson the eminence of being the strongest women writers in the English language.

III

Henry James asserted that *"Middlemarch* is at once one of the strongest and one of the weakest of English novels." The second half of that judgment was evidently defensive. By common consent, *Middlemarch* is equal, at least, to any other novel in the language. Dorothea Brooke is a crucial figure in that great sequence of the fictive heroines of the Protestant Will that includes Clarissa Harlowe, Elizabeth Bennet, Emma Woodhouse, Esther Summerson, Hester Prynne, Isabel Archer, Ursula Brangwen, and Clarissa Dalloway, among others. James complained that "Dorothea was altogether too superb a heroine to be wasted; yet she plays a narrower part than the imagination of the reader demands." Yet this is surely true of Isabel Archer also, since, like Dorothea Brooke, "she is of more consequence than the action of which she is the nominal centre." It could be argued that only Hester Prynne is provided with an action worthy of her, but then the superb Hester is called upon mostly to suffer. Dimmesdale, under any circumstances, seems as inadequate for Hester as Will Ladislaw seems too inconsequential for Dorothea, or as even Ralph Touchett seems weak in relation to Isabel. Except for Clarissa Harlowe confronting her equally strong agonist in Lovelace, the heroines of the Protestant Will are always involved with men less memorable than themselves. Lawrence attempted to defy this tradition, but failed, as we must acknowledge when we set the tendentious Birkin beside the vital Ursula.

"Of course she gets up spurious miracles," the young Yeats remarked in defense of Madame Blavatsky, "but what *is* a woman of genius to do in the Nineteenth Century?" What is Saint Theresa to do in the nineteenth century, and in England, of all countries? What is Isabel Archer, heiress of all the ages, to do in the nineteenth century? In America, is she to marry Caspar Goodwood, a prospect that neither she nor James can endure? In Europe, she marries the subtly dreadful Osmond, mock-Emersonian and pseudo-Paterian. Even Casaubon might have been better, George Eliot could have been sly enough to tell Henry James. The heroes of the Protestant Will may have existed in mere fact—witness Oliver Cromwell and John Milton—but they have not been persuasively represented in prose fiction.

Rereading *Middlemarch* makes me unhappy only when I have to contemplate Will Ladislaw, an idealized portrait of George Henry Lewes,
George Eliot's not unworthy lover. Otherwise, the novel compels aesthetic awe in me, if only because it alone, among novels, raises moral reflection to the level of high art. There is Nietzsche of course, but then *Zarathustra* is not a novel, and *Zarathustra* is an aesthetic disaster anyway. The
great moralists, from Montaigne through Emerson to Freud, do not write
prose fiction, and yet George Eliot is of their company. If we can speak
aesthetically of the Moral Sublime, then she must help inform our speaking. All versions of the Sublime seem to involve a surrender of easier pleasures in favor of more difficult pleasures, but the Moral Sublime, in Freud
or George Eliot, necessarily centers upon a coming to terms with the reality principle.

How is it that Eliot can imbue her moralizings with an aesthetic authority, when such contemporary practitioners as Doris Lessing, Walker
Percy, and even Iris Murdoch cannot? I think that there are two answers
here, and they may be quite unrelated to one another. One is that Eliot is
unmatched among all other novelists in cognitive strength; she has the
same eminence in prose fiction as Emily Dickinson has in lyric poetry or
Shakespeare in the drama. We ordinarily do not estimate imaginative writers in terms of intellect, but that may be one of the eternal weaknesses of
Western literary criticism. And yet the puzzle is great. Walt Whitman, in
my judgment, surpasses even Dickinson among American poets, yet compared to her he cannot think at all. Dickinson and George Eliot, like
Blake, rethink everything in earth and in heaven for themselves, as Shakespeare, above all writers, would appear to have done for himself. Such
cognitive originality clearly does become an aesthetic value, in combination with other modes of mastery, yet it scarcely exists in poets as superb
as Whitman and Tennyson.

Unallied to her cognitive strength (so far as I can tell) is Eliot's other
massive aesthetic advantage as a moralist: a lack of any of the crippling
intensities of the wrong kind of self-consciousness concerning morals and
moralization. We do not encounter hesitation or affectation in Eliot's
broodings upon moral dilemmas. She contrives to be at once intricate and
direct in such matters, as in the famous conclusion to *Middlemarch*:

> Certainly those determining acts of her life were not ideally
> beautiful. They were the mixed result of young and noble im-
> pulse struggling amidst the conditions of an imperfect social
> state, in which great feelings will often take the aspect of error,
> and great faith the aspect of illusion. For there is no creature

whose inward being is so strong that it is not greatly determined by what lies outside it. A new Theresa will hardly have the opportunity of reforming a conventual life, any more than a new Antigone will spend her heroic piety in daring all for the sake of a brother's burial: the medium in which their ardent deeds took shape is for ever gone. But we insignificant people with our daily words and acts are preparing the lives of many Dorotheas, some of which may present a far sadder sacrifice than that of the Dorothea whose story we know.

Her finely-touched spirit had still its fine issues, though they were not widely visible. Her full nature, like that river of which Cyrus broke the strength, spent itself in channels which had no great name on the earth. But the effect of her being on those around her was incalculably diffusive: for the growing good of the world is partly dependent on unhistoric acts; and that things are not so ill with you and me as they might have been, is half owing to the number who lived faithfully a hidden life, and rest in unvisited tombs.

Eliot is defending both of Dorothea's marriages, but I rapidly forget Dorothea, at least for a while, when I read and ponder that massive third sentence, at once a truism and a profound moment of wisdom writing: "For there is no creature whose inward being is so strong that it is not greatly determined by what lies outside it." Our overdetermination—by society, by generational position, by the familial past—could not be better expressed, nor could we be better reminded that we ourselves will overdetermine those who come after us, even heroines as intense as Saint Theresa, Antigone, and Dorothea Brooke.

Eliot's proleptic answer to Henry James's protest at the waste of the superb Dorothea is centered in one apothegm: "the growing good of the world is partly dependent on unhistoric acts." James might have agreed, but then would have murmured that the growing good of the world and of the art of fiction are somewhat different matters. It is George Eliot's peculiar strength that she comes closer than any other novelist to persuading us that the good of the world and of the novel are ultimately reconcilable.

Optic and Semiotic
in *Middlemarch*

J. Hillis Miller

> . . . *this power of generalising which gives men so much the superiority in mistake over the dumb animals.*
>
> GEORGE ELIOT, *Middlemarch*

George Eliot's apparent aim in *Middlemarch* (1871–72) is to present a total picture of provincial society in England at the period just before the first Reform Bill of 1832. She also wants to interpret this picture totally. She wants both to show what is there and to show how it works. This enterprise of totalization, as one might call it, is shared with an important group of other masterworks of Victorian fiction, including Thackeray's *Vanity Fair* (1847–48), Dickens's *Bleak House* (1852–53), *Little Dorrit* (1855–57), and *Our Mutual Friend* (1864–65), and Trollope's *The Way We Live Now* (1874–75). All these novels have many characters and employ multiple analogous plots. They cast a wide net and aim at inclusiveness, in part by a method of accumulation. Nevertheless, since the actual societies in question were unmanageably complex and multitudinous, some strategy of compression, of economy, had to be devised in each case. As George Meredith puts it in the prelude to *The Egoist,* "the inward mirror, the embracing and condensing spirit, is required to give us those interminable mile-post piles of matter . . . in essence, in chosen samples, digestibly." The means of condensation used vary considerably, however, from novelist to novelist.

Dickens, for example, achieves inclusiveness by making the part explicitly stand for the whole. He emphasizes the synecdochic, representa-

---

From *The Worlds of Victorian Fiction* (Harvard English Studies 6). © 1975 by the President and Fellows of Harvard College. Harvard University Press, 1975.

tive, emblematic quality of his characters. Mr. Krook, the rag and bottle shopkeeper in *Bleak House,* stands for the lord chancellor, his shop for the Court of Chancery. Chancery, in turn, is a synecdoche for the state of "wiglomeration" of English society as a whole. In the same novel, Sir Leicester Dedlock is presented as an example of the whole class of aristocrats; Gridley, the Man from Shropshire, is an emblem for all the suitors who are destroyed by the delays of Chancery, and so on. Moreover, the range of examples includes by this method of synecdoche all of England. Characters from the country and from the city, from the lowest level of society to the highest, are presented.

George Eliot is more straightforwardly "realistic" in her procedure. *Middlemarch* presents a large group of the sort of people one would in fact have been likely to find in a provincial town in the Midlands. Their representative or symbolic quality is not insisted upon. This would be the wrong track to follow, I believe, in a search for her methods of totalization. Moreover, Eliot does not present examples from the whole range of English society. The relation of Middlemarch to English society is rather that of part to whole, or that of a sample to the whole cloth, according to a metaphor I shall be examining later. The relationship is once more synecdochic, but the kind of synecdoche in question is different from the one used by Dickens. In *Bleak House* the member of a class is presented as a "symbol" of the whole class. In *Middlemarch* a fragment is examined as a "sample" of the larger whole of which it is a part, though the whole impinges on the part as the "medium" within which it lives, as national politics affect Middlemarch when there is a general election, or as the coming of the railroad upsets rural traditions. Eliot's strategy of totalization is to present individual character or event in the context of that wider medium and to affirm universal laws of human behavior in terms of characters whose specificity and even uniqueness is indicated by the completeness of the psychological portraits of each—Dorothea, Lydgate, Casaubon, Bulstrode, Fred Vincy, Mary Garth, and the rest. This fullness of characterization and the accompanying circumstantiality of social detail in *Middlemarch* have been deservedly admired. They make this novel perhaps the masterwork of Victorian realism.

The subtitle of *Middlemarch* is *A Study of Provincial Life.* This may put the novel under the aegis of a kind of painting, a "study from life." The more powerful association of the word, however, is with a scientific "study." In *Middlemarch* Eliot is attempting to fulfill for the life of a provincial town that enterprise she had mapped out in her important early essay on the German sociologist of peasant life, Wilhelm Heinrich von

Riehl. In that essay, "The Natural History of German Life" (*Westminster Review*, 1856), she had implicitly proposed the writing of works of fiction which would do for English life what Riehl had done for the German peasant: "Art is the nearest thing to life: it is a mode of amplifying experience and extending our contact with our fellow-men beyond the bounds of our personal lot. All the more sacred is the task of the artist when he undertakes to paint the life of the People. Falsification here is far more pernicious than in the more artificial aspects of life." Much of *Middlemarch* is modeled on the sociologist's respect for individual fact George Eliot so praises in this essay. The experience of each character in *Middlemarch* is described in such detail that the reader is encouraged not to forget its differences from the experiences of the other characters.

Nevertheless, the narrator of *Middlemarch* assumes throughout that the behavior of these unique people manifests certain general and universal laws. These laws may be formulated and are in fact constantly formulated, as when the narrator says: "We are all of us born in moral stupidity, taking the world as an udder to feed our supreme selves." The special mode of totalization in *Middlemarch* is this combination of specificity, on the one hand, and, on the other hand, generalizing interpretation on the basis of specificity. Such generalizing is proposed as valid not just for all people in the particular middle-class society of Middlemarch, and not just for the English society at a specific moment of its history of which Middlemarch is a part, but for all people in all cultures in all times.

I intend here to explore one more of this generalizing interpretation, the presentation by the narrator of certain all-encompassing metaphors which are proposed as models for Middlemarch society. Such metaphors are put forward as a means of thinking of all the people in Middlemarch in their interrelations through time. Each metaphor is an interpretative net which the reader is invited to cast over the whole society, to use as a paradigm by means of which to think of the whole. I shall argue that there are three such totalizing metaphors, or rather families of metaphors. Each group of metaphors is related to the others, fulfilling them, but at the same time contradicting them, canceling them out, or undermining their validity.

The recurrence of such metaphors throughout *Middlemarch* and their assumed validity affirms one of the most important presuppositions of the novel. The unique life of each of the characters is presented as part of a single system of complex interaction in time and space. No man, for Eliot, lives alone. Each exists in "the same embroiled medium, the same troublous fitfully-illuminated life" (chap. 30). The nature of this "medium" and of the interaction of character with character within it is analyzed throughout by the narrator. The voice of the narrator, sympathetic certainly, but also clairvoyant in his insight into human folly, is in *Middlemarch,* as in Victorian novels generally, the most immediate presence for the reader and the chief generating force behind the stylistic texture of the novel.

> text . . . from Medieval Latin *textus,* (Scriptural) text, from Latin, literary composition, "woven thing," from the past participle of *texere,* to weave.

Perhaps the most salient totalizing metaphor presented as a model for the community of Middlemarch is in fact a family of related metaphors. Each member of this family compares Middlemarch society or some part of it to a spatially or temporally deployed material complex—a labyrinth, or flowing water, or woven cloth. There are two important implications of these metaphors as they are used in the novel. The first is the assumption that a society is in some way like a material field and therefore is open to the same kind of objective scientific investigation as may be applied to such a field, for example, to flowing water. The other is the assumption, reinforced by many passages in the novel, that the structure or texture of small-scale pieces of the whole is the same as the structure or texture of the whole and so may be validly described with the same figures. This is the assumption of the validity of one kind of synecdoche. The part is "really like" the whole, and an investigation of a sample will lead to valid conclusions about the whole. If Middlemarch society as a whole is like flowing water or like woven cloth, the mental life of each of its inhabitants may also be validly described in the same metaphors. In a similar way, when the reader or the narrator focuses on the relation between two of the characters out of the whole lot, the metaphors will be found to be valid on that scale too. In the other direction, as I have suggested, it is implied that what is true in Middlemarch is also true for English society as a whole, or even for any human life anywhere and at any time. *Middlemarch* is full of such shifts in perspective from close up to far away and back to close up again, according to that law of scientific method which Lydgate admirably formulates: "there must be a systole and diastole in all inquiry," and "a man's mind must be continually expanding and shrinking between the whole human horizon and the horizon of an object-glass" (chap. 63). Eliot's assumption is that in the social world, at least, such changes in scale reveal a strict homogeneity between the large-scale and small-scale grain or texture of things. As Will Ladislaw phrases it, "the little waves make the large ones and are of the same pattern" (chap. 46).

The most persistent of these structural metaphors, as has often been noticed, is the metaphor of the web. One explicit application of the image of a web to the whole range of social relationships in the novel comes in the passage where the narrator distinguishes his [her?] enterprise from that of Fielding [after all, the fiction of the male narrator is still maintained in *Middlemarch*. To speak of the narrator as a "he" allows the reader to keep firmly in mind the distinction between the author of the novel, Marian Evans, and the created role of the storyteller, George Eliot]. Whereas Fielding lived in more spacious times and could allow himself the luxury of the famous "copious remarks and digressions," "I at least," says the narrator, "have so much to do in unravelling certain human lots, and seeing how they were woven and interwoven, that all the light I can command must be concentrated on this particular web, and not dispersed over that tempting range of relevancies called the universe" (chap. 15). The narrator's effort is not merely that of observation. He must, like a good scientist, take apart the specimen being analyzed, unravel all its fibers to see how it is put together, how it has been woven and interwoven. That the texture of Middlemarch society as a whole may be accurately represented in a metaphor of woven cloth is taken for granted throughout the novel. It appears in many apparently casual texts as a reinforcement of more elaborate passages inviting the reader to keep the paradigm of the web before his mind. Lydgate, to give one example from early in the novel, finds himself for the first time "feeling the hampering threadlike pressure of small social conditions, and their frustrating complexity" (chap. 18).

The metaphor of a web, however, is also used repeatedly in *Middlemarch* to describe the texture of smaller-scale entities within the larger social fabric. The lovemaking of Rosamond and Lydgate, for example, is described as the collective weaving of an intersubjective tissue:

> Young love-making—that gossamer web! Even the points it clings to—the things whence its subtle interlacings are swung— are scarcely perceptible; momentary touches of finger-tips, meetings of rays from blue and dark orbs, unfinished phrases, lightest changes of cheek and lip, faintest tremors. The web itself is made of spontaneous beliefs and indefinable joys, yearnings of one life towards another, visions of completeness, indefinite trust. And Lydgate fell to spinning that web from his inward self with wonderful rapidity . . . As for Rosamond, she

was in the water-lily's expanding wonderment at its own fuller
life, and she too was spinning industriously at the mutual web.

Another important use of the metaphor of a web is made in the description of Lydgate's scientific researches. Lydgate's attempt to find the
"primitive tissue" is based on the assumption that the metaphor of woven
cloth applies in the organic as well as in the social realm. His use of the
figure brings into the open the parallelism between Eliot's aim as a sociologist of provincial life and the aims of contemporary biologists. Lydgate's
research is based on the hypothesis that all the organs of the body are dif-
ferentiations of "certain primary webs or tissues": "have not these structures some common basis from which they have all started, as your sars-
net, gauze, net, satin and velvet from the raw cocoon?" (chap. 15). If
Lydgate assumes that biological entities may be described as tissues, the
narrator of *Middlemarch* makes the same assumptions about the subjective
lives of the characters. Of Lydgate, for example, the narrator says that
"momentary speculations as to all the possible grounds for Mrs. Bulstrode's hints had managed to get woven like slight clinging hairs into the
more substantial web of his thoughts" (chap. 31). Much later in the novel,
basing the generalization again on Lydgate's psychology, the narrator asks:
"Is it not rather what we expect in men, that they should have numerous
strands of experience lying side by side and never compare them with each
other?" (chap. 58). This image of mental or intersubjective life as a reticu-
lated pattern like a grid is implicit when a few pages earlier the narrator
says of Rosamond and Lydgate that "between him and her indeed there
was that total missing of each other's mental track, which is too evidently
possible even between persons who are continually thinking of each
other." The image of mental or social life as traveling along tracks which
may or may not intersect with others is also latent in an earlier remark
about Ladislaw: "There are characters which are continually creating colli-
sions and nodes for themselves in dramas which nobody is prepared to act
with them."

To the metaphor of the web, however, must be added the metaphor
of the stream. Collective or individual life in Middlemarch is not a fixed
pattern like a carpet. The web is always in movement. The pervasive figure for this is that of flowing water. This figure is homogeneous with the
figure of the web in that flowing water, for Eliot, is seen as made up of
currents, filaments flowing side by side, intermingling and dividing. Flowing water is, so to speak, a temporalized web. Casaubon, for example, is
said, in a fine series of phrases, to have possessed "that proud narrow sen-
sitiveness which has not mass enough to spare for transformation into

sympathy, and quivers thread-like in small currents of self-preoccupation or at best of an egoistic scrupulosity" (chap. 29). Lydgate, after he has met Rosamond, "had no sense that any new current had set into his life" (chap. 16). Of his life as a whole when it is in the midst of being lived (in the middle of its march, as one might say), the narrator asserts that it has "the complicated probabilities of an arduous purpose, with all the possible thwartings and furtherings of circumstance, all the niceties of inward balance, by which a man swims and makes his point or else is carried headlong," for "character too is a process and an unfolding" (chap. 15). In another place, the narrator speaks of "the chief current" of Dorothea's anxiety (chap. 22), and, as opposed to the egotistic scrupulosity of Casaubon's small soul, "in Dorothea's mind there was a current into which all thought and feeling were apt sooner or later to flow—the reaching forward of the whole consciousness towards the fullest truth, the least partial good" (chap. 20). In the climactic scene of Dorothea's renunciation of her fortune to marry Will, "the flood of her young passion bear[s] down all the obstructions which had kept her silent" (chap. 83).

One final element must be added to complete the description of Eliot's admirable development of a quasi-scientific model to describe the subjective life of the individual, the relations of two persons within the social "medium," and the nature of that medium as a whole. This element has already been anticipated in what has been said about the correspondence, in Eliot's view of things, between small- and large-scale structures. This idea, however, is but one aspect of a larger assumption, that is, the notion that any process in any of the three "scales" is made up of endlessly subdividable "minutiae." Anything that we call a "unit" or a single fact, in social or in mental life, is not single but multiple. A finer lens would always make smaller parts visible. The smaller parts, in turn, are made up of even smaller entities.

One corollary of this vision of things is the rejection of that straightforward idea of single causes which had characterized, for example, *Adam Bede*. In *Middlemarch* Eliot still believes in causality, but in the psychological and social realms the causes are now seen as unimaginably multiple. No fact is in itself single, and no fact is explicable by a single relationship to a single cause. Each fact is a kind of multitudinous node which exists only arbitrarily as a single thing because we happen to have the microscope focused as we do. If the focus were finer, the apparently single fact would subdivide and reveal itself to be made of multiple minutiae. If the focus were coarser the fact would disappear within the larger entity of which it is a part. A single momentary state of mind, for example, exists in relation to all its latent motives, the minutiae of mental life which underlie it, in relation also to its own past and future, and in multiple relation to what is outside it, all the other people to whom the person is socially related. The metaphor of the variable lens of a microscope is in fact used by Eliot to make this point:

> Even with a microscope directed on a water-drop we find ourselves making interpretations which turn out to be rather coarse; for whereas under a weak lens you may seem to see a creature exhibiting an active voracity into which other smaller creatures actively play as if they were so many animated tax-pennies, a stronger lens reveals to you certain tiniest hairlets which make vortices for these victims while the swallower waits passively at his receipt of custom.
>
> (chap. 6)

One might ask, parenthetically, how and why the metaphor of the microscope has been contaminated here by another apparently unrelated metaphor, that of money, taxes, and "custom." This interpretation of one metaphor by another metaphor is characteristic of Eliot's use of figure. An attempt to explain fully this linguistic habit must be postponed, but one can say that the displacement of one figure by another is asymmetrically parallel to the displacement of the weak lens by the strong lens of the microscope. In each case, one vision of things is replaced by another. The optical visions are apparently reconcilable, whereas the two metaphors interfere with one another even if they are not wholly contradictory. The text of *Middlemarch,* in any case, goes on to apply the metaphor of the double-lensed microscope to a particular case in the novel: "In this way, metaphorically speaking, a strong lens applied to Mrs. Cadwallader's matchmaking will show a play of minute causes producing what may be called thought and speech vortices to bring her the sort of food she needed."

The phrase "play of minute causes" is echoed throughout the novel by similar phrases keeping before the reader the idea that the mental and social events being described are extremely complex. This complexity is essential to their mode of existence. The narrator speaks, for example, of "a slow preparation of effects from one life on another" (chap. 11), or of an ardor which cooled "imperceptibly," like other youthful loves ("Nothing in the world more subtle than the process of their gradual change!" chap. 15), or of "the minutiae of mental make in which one of us differs from another" (chap. 15), or of Lydgate's "testing vision of details and relations" (chap. 16), or of "the suppressed transitions which unite all contrasts (chap. 20), or of the "nice distinctions of rank in Middlemarch" (chap. 23), or of "the living myriad of hidden suckers whereby the belief and the conduct are wrought into mutual sustainment" (chap. 53), or of a "fact" which "was broken into little sequences" (chap. 61), or of the way Bulstrode's "misdeeds were like the subtle muscular movements which are not taken account of in the consciousness" (chap. 68).

All this family of intertwined metaphors and motifs—the web, the current, the minutely subdivided entity—make up a single comprehensive model or picture of Middlemarch society as being a complex moving medium, tightly interwoven into a single fabric, always in process, endlessly subdividable. This medium can be seen and studied objectively, as if there could be an ideal observer who does not change what he observes and who sees the moving web as it were from all perspectives at once, from close up and far away, with both gross and fine lenses, in a continual systole and diastole in inquiry. The storyteller in *Middlemarch* is in short the ideal observer of Victorian fiction, the "omniscient" narrator. His aim is to do full representative justice to the complexity of the condition of man in his social medium. There are many admirable passages in *Middlemarch* giving examples of what the narrator sees, each a new application of the model I have been describing. None is perhaps so comprehensive an exploitation of the totalizing implications of this family of metaphors as an admirable passage in chapter 11 describing "old provincial society":

> Old provincial society had its share of this subtle movement: had not only its striking downfalls, its brilliant young professional dandies who ended by living up an entry with a drab and six children for their establishment, but also those less marked vicissitudes which are constantly shifting the boundaries of social intercourse, and begetting new consciousness of interdependence. Some slipped a little downward, some got higher footing: people denied aspirates, gained wealth, and fastidious gentlemen stood for boroughs; some were caught in political currents, some in ecclesiastical, and perhaps found themselves surprisingly grouped in consequence; while a few personages or families that stood with rocky firmness amid all this fluctuation, were slowly presenting new aspects in spite of solidity, and altering with the double change of self and beholder.

> Therefore speak I to them in parables: because they seeing see not; and hearing they hear not, neither do they understand.
> (Matt. 13:13)

> er hat das Auge nicht dafür, das Einmalige zu sehen; die Ähnlichseherei und Gleichmacherei ist das Merkmal schwacher Augen. [Friedrich Nietzsche, *Die Fröhliche Wissenshaft,* para.

228, in *Werke,* ed. Karl Schlecta (Munich: Carl Hanser Verlag, 1966), 2:152–53: "they lack eyes for seeing what is unique. Seeing things as similar and making things the same is the sign of weak eyes" (*The Gay Science,* trans. Walter Kaufmann [New York: Vintage Books, 1974], p. 212).]

"Double change of self and beholder"! I have said that my first family of metaphors in *Middlemarch* does not raise problems of perspective, or that in any case it presupposes the possibility of an ideal observer such as that assumed in much nineteenth-century science, in the days before operationalism, relativity, and the principle of indeterminacy. This is true, but in fact an optical or epistemological metaphor has already introduced itself surreptitiously into many of my examples. The narrator must concentrate "all the light [he] can command" (chap. 15) on his particular web in order to see clearly how it is woven. Study of the web requires constant changes of the lens in the systole and diastole of inquiry. Any conceivable observer in Middlemarch will be changing himself along with all the other changes and so will change what he sees.

A pervasive figure for the human situation in *Middlemarch* is that of the seer who must try to identify clearly what is present before him. This metaphor contaminates the apparently clear-cut objectivist implications of the metaphor of the flowing web. As more and more examples of it accumulate, it struggles with a kind of imperialistic will to power over the whole to replace that objectivism with a fully developed subjectivism or perspectivism. The "omniscience" of the narrator, according to this alternative model for the human condition, can be obtained only because he is able to share the points of view of all the characters, thereby transcending the limited vision of any single person. "In watching effects," as the narrator says, "if only of an electric battery, it is often necessary to change our place and examine a particular mixture or group at some distance from the point where the movement we are interested in was set up" (chap. 40). The narrator can move in imagination from one vantage point to another, or from close up to far away. He can be, like the angel Uriel, "watching the progress of planetary history from the Sun" (chap. 41), and at the same time share in that microscopic vision of invisible process, perceptible only to inward imaginative vision, so splendidly described in a passage about Lydgate's method as a scientist. It is a passage which also describes covertly the claims of Eliot's own fictional imagination. Lydgate, the narrator says, is endowed

with the imagination that reveals subtle actions inaccessible by any sort of lens, but tracked in that outer darkness through long pathways of necessary sequence by the inward light which is the last refinement of Energy, capable of bathing even the ethereal atoms in its ideally illumined space . . . he was enamoured of that arduous invention which is the very eye of research, provisionally framing its object and correcting it to more and more exactness of relation; he wanted to pierce the obscurity of those minute processes which prepare human misery and joy.

(chap. 16)

The metaphor of the complex moving web, the "embroiled medium," is, one can see, further complicated, or even contradicted, by the metaphor of vision. Each of those nodes in the social web which is a separate human being is endowed with a power to see the whole. This power is defined throughout the novel as essentially distorting. Each man or woman has a "centre of self, whence the lights and shadows must always fall with a certain difference" (chap. 21). The "radiance" of Dorothea's "transfigured girlhood," as the narrator says, "fell on the first object that came within its level" (chap. 5). Her mistakes, as her sister Celia tells her, are errors in seeing, of which her literal myopia is a metonymy. "I thought it right to tell you," says Celia apropos of the fact that Sir James intends to propose to Dorothea, "because you went on as you always do, never looking just where you are, and treading in the wrong place. You always see what nobody else sees; it is impossible to satisfy you; yet you never see what is quite plain" (chap. 4). Mr. Casaubon, however, is also "the centre of his own world." From that point of view he is "liable to think that others were providentially made for him, and especially to consider them in the light of their fitness for the author of a "Key to all Mythologies" (chap. 10). Of the inhabitants of Middlemarch generally it can in fact be said that each makes of what he sees something determined by his own idosyncratic perspective, for "Probabilities are as various as the faces to be seen at will on fretwork or paperhangings: every form is there, from Jupiter to Judy, if you only look with creative inclination" (chap. 32).

Seeing, then, is for Eliot not a neutral, objective, dispassionate, or passive act. It is the creative projection of light from an egotistic center motivated by desire and need. This projected radiance orders the field of vision according to the presuppositions of the seer. The act of seeing is the spontaneous affirmation of a will to power over what is seen. This affirmation of order is based on the instinctive desire to believe that the world is providentially structured in a neat pattern of which one is oneself the center, for "we are all of us born in moral stupidity, taking the world as an udder to feed our supreme selves." This interpretation of the act of seeing is most fully presented in the admirable and often discussed "parable" of the "pier-glass" at the beginning of chapter 27:

> An eminent philosopher among my friends, who can dignify even your ugly furniture by lifting it into the serene light of science, has shown me this pregnant little fact. Your pier-glass or extensive survace of polished steel made to be rubbed by a housemaid, will be minutely and multitudinously scratched in all directions; but place now against it a lighted candle as a centre of illumination, and lo! the scratches will seem to arrange themselves in a fine series of concentric circles round that little sun. It is demonstrable that the scratches are going everywhere impartially, and it is only your candle which produces the flattering illusion of a concentric arrangement, its light falling with an exclusive optical selection. These things are a parable. The scratches are events, and the candle is the egoism of any person now absent—of Miss Vincy, for example. Rosamond had a Providence of her own who had kindly made her more charming than other girls, and who seemed to have arranged Fred's illness and Mr. Wrench's mistake in order to bring her and Lydgate within effective proximity.

This passage is perhaps more complicated than it at first appears. It begins with an example of what it describes, an example which implicitly takes note of the fact that Eliot's own "parabolic" method, in this text, as in many other passages in *Middlemarch,* is a seeing of one thing in the "light" of another. The word "parable," like the word "allegory," the word "metaphor," or indeed all terms for figures of speech, is of course itself based on a figure. It means "to set beside," from the Greek *para,* beside, and *balletin,* to throw. A parable is set or thrown at some distance from the meaning which controls it and to which it obliquely or parabolically refers, as a parabolic curve is controlled, across a space, by its parallelism to a line on the cone of which it is a section. The line and the cone may have only a virtual or imaginary existence, as in the case of a comet with a parabolic course. The parabola creates that line in the empty air, just as the parables of Jesus remedy a defect of vision, give sight to the blind, and make the invisible visible. In Eliot's parable of the pier glass the "eminent philosopher" transfigures "ugly furniture," a pier glass, by "lifting it into the serene light of science," but also makes an obscure scientific principle visible. In the same way, the candle makes the random scratches on the pier glass appear to be concentric circles, and so Rosamond interprets what happens around her as being governed by her private providence, just as Eliot sees provincial society as like a woven web, or the ego of an individual person in the light of a comparison to a candle. The same projective, subjective, even egotistic act, seeing one thing as set or thrown, parabolically, beside another, is involved in all four cases.

At this point the reader may remember that the narrator, in a passage I earlier took as a "key" expression of Eliot's use of a model of objective scientific observation, says "all the light I can command must be concentrated on this particular web." With a slight change of formulation this could be seen as implying that the subjective source of light not only illuminates what is seen but also, as in the case of the candle held to the pier glass, determines the structure of what is seen. Middlemarch society perhaps appears to be a web only because a certain kind of subjective light is concentrated on it. The passage taken in isolation does not say this, but its near congruence with the passage about the pier glass, a slightly asymmetrical analogy based on the fact that the same metaphorical elements are present in each allows the contradictory meaning to seep into the passage about the web when the two texts are set side by side. Each is seen as a modulation of the other. The same key would not open both, though a "master key" might.

In spite of the disquieting possibilities generated by resonances between two similar but not quite congruent passages, the narrator in various ways throughout *Middlemarch* is clearly claiming to be able to transcend the limitations of the self-centered ego by seeing things impersonally, objectively, scientifically: "It is demonstrable that the scratches are going everywhere impartially." This objective vision, such is the logic of Eliot's parable, shows that what is "really there" has no order whatsoever, but is merely random scratches without pattern or meaning. The pier glass is "minutely and multitudinously scratched in all directions." The idea that reality is chaotic, without intrinsic order or form, and the corollary that any order it may appear to have is projected illicitly by some patterning ego, would seem to be contradicted by the series of totalizing metaphors I have explored—web, flowing water, and so on—as well as by the generalizing, rationalizing, order-finding activity of the narrator throughout the book. It would seem hardly plausible, at this point at least, to say that reality for Eliot is a chaotic disorder. It might seem more likely that this is an irrelevant implication of the parable, an implication which has by accident, as it were, slipped in along with implications which are "intended." A decision about this must be postponed.

Among the "intended" implications, however, may be one arising from the fact that a pier glass is a kind of mirror, while the examples of the "flattering illusion" Eliot would have encountered in Herbert Spencer or in Ruskin lacked this feature. Ruskin, for example, speaks of the path of reflected moonlight seen across the surface of a lake by a spectator on the shore. The pier glass would, after all, reflect what was brought near it, as well as produce its own interfering illusion of concentric circles, and the candle is a displacement or parable for the ego, of Rosamond or whomever. Rosamond would of course see her own image in the mirror, Narcissus-like. This implication of the parable links it with all those other passages, not only in *Middlemarch* but also in *Adam Bede,* for example, or in *Daniel Deronda,* where egotism is symbolized by the admiration of one's image in a mirror, or where the work of representation is expressed in the traditional image of holding a mirror up to reality. A passage in chapter 10, for example, apropos of the low opinion of Mr. Casaubon held by his neighbors, says that even "the greatest man of his age" could not escape "unfavourable reflections of himself in various small mirrors." This apparently uses the figure of the mirror in a way contradicting the parable of the pier glass. The mirror is now the ego rather than the external world. In fact, however, what is always in question when the mirror appears is narcissistic self-reflection. This may be thought of as seeing our own reflection in the mirroring would outside because we have projected it there. Or it may be thought of as our distortion of the world outside in our reflecting ego, so that it takes the configurations of our private vision of things. Any two subjectivities, according to this model, will face one another like confronting mirrors. If Casaubon was "the centre of his own world," had "an equivalent centre of self, whence the lights and shadows must always fall with a certain difference," the people in whom he seeks the reflection of his own sense of himself are not innocent mirrors, but are themselves instruments of distortion: "even Milton, looking for his portrait in a spoon, must submit to have the facial angle of a bumpkin" (chap. 10). The projection of one's selfish needs or desires on reality orders that random set of events into a pattern, the image of the mirror would imply. This pattern is in fact a portrait of the ego itself, an objective embodiment of its subjective configurations. The terrible isolation of each person, for Eliot, lies in the way each goes through the world encountering only himself, his own image reflected back to him by the world because he (or she) has put it there in the first place, in the illusory interpretation of the world the person spontaneously makes.

The narrator of *Middlemarch,* it would seem, can escape from this fate only by using perspective to transcend perspective, by moving from the microscopic close-up to the panoramic distant view, and by shifting constantly from the point of view of one character to the point of view of another. Such shifts will give a full multidimensional picture of what is "really there," as when the narrator, after a prolonged immersion within the subjective experience of Dorothea, asks: "—but why always Dorothea? Was her point of view the only possible one with regard to this marriage? I protest against all our interest, all our efforts at understanding being given to the young skins that look blooming in spite of trouble . . . In spite of the blinking eyes and white moles objectionable to Celia, and the want of muscular curve which was morally painful to Sir James, Mr. Casaubon had an intense consciousness within him, and was spiritually a-hungered like the rest of us" (chap. 29).

The word "interpretation," however, which I used just above, will serve as a clue indicating the presence within the optical metaphors of an element so far not identified as such. This element contaminates and ultimately subverts the optical model in the same way that the optical model contaminates and makes more problematic the images of the web or of the current. All the optical passages in fact contain elements which show that for Eliot seeing is never "merely" optical. Seeing is never simply a matter of identifying correctly what is seen, seeing that windmills are not giants, a washpan a washpan and not a helmet of Mambrino, to use the example from *Don Quixote* cited as an epigraph for chapter 2. Seeing is always interpretation, that is, what is seen is always taken as a sign standing for something else, as an emblem, a hieroglyph, a parable.

Superimposed on the models for the human situation of the objective scientist and the subjective perspectivist, interlaced with them, overlapping them in each of their expressions, is a model for the situation of the characters and of the narrator which says all human beings in all situations are like readers of a text. Moreover, if for Eliot all seeing is falsified by the limitations of point of view, it is an even more inevitable law, for her, that we make things what they are by naming them in one way or another, that is, by the incorporation of empirical data into a conventional system of signs. A corollary of this law is the fact that all interpretation of signs is false interpretation. The original naming was an act of interpretation which falsified. The reading of things made into signs is necessarily a further falsification, an interpretation of an interpretation. An important sequence of passages running like Ariadne's thread though the labyrinthine verbal complexity of *Middlemarch* develops a subtle theory of signs and of interpretation. Along with this goes a recognition of the irreducibly figurative or metaphorical nature of all language.

I have elsewhere discussed George Eliot's theory of signs, of interpretation, and of figurative language in *Middlemarch*. Limitations of space would in any case forbid discussion of this third model for the human situation here. It is possible, however, to conclude on the basis of what I have said about two families of metaphors in *Middlemarch* that the models are multiple and incompatible. They are incompatible not in the sense that one is more primitive or naive and gives way to a more sophisticated paradigm, but in the sense that any passage will reveal itself when examined closely to be the battleground of conflicting metaphors. This incoherent, heterogeneous, "unreadable," or nonsynthesizable quality of the text of *Middlemarch* jeopardizes the narrator's effort of totalization. It suggests that one gets a different kind of totality depending on what metaphorical model is used. The presence of several incompatible models brings into the open the arbitrary and partial character of each and so ruins the claim of the narrator to have a total, unified, and impartial vision. What is true for the characters of *Middlemarch,* that "we all of us, grave or light, get our thoughts entangled in metaphors, and act fatally on the strength of them" (chap. 10), must also be true for the narrator. The web of interpretative figures cast by the narrator over the characters of the story becomes a net in which the narrator himself is entangled and trapped, his sovereign vision blinded.

George Eliot's insight into the dismaying dangers of metaphor is expressed already in an admirably witty and perceptive passage in *The Mill on the Floss,* published over a decade before *Middlemarch,* in 1860. Here already she formulates her recognition of the deconstructive powers of figurative language, its undoing of any attempt to make a complete, and completely coherent, picture of human life. This undoing follows from the fact that if we can seldom say what a thing is without saying it is something else, without speaking parabolically, then there is no way to avoid the ever present possibility of altering the meaning by altering the metaphor:

> It is astonishing what a different result one gets by changing the metaphor! Once call the brain an intellectual stomach, and one's ingenious conception of the classics and geometry as ploughs and harrows seems to settle nothing. But then it is open to some one else to follow great authorities, and call the mind a sheet of white paper or a mirror, in which case one's knowledge of the digestive process becomes quite irrelevant. It was doubtless an ingenious idea to call the camel the ship of the desert, but it would hardly lead one far in training that useful

beast. O Aristotle! if you had had the advantage of being "the freshest modern" instead of the greatest ancient, would you not have mingled your praise of metaphorical speech, as a sign of high intelligence, with a lamentation that intelligence so rarely shows itself in speech without metaphor—that we can so seldom declare what a thing is, except by saying it is something else?

M*iddlemarch:* Public and Private Worlds

Barbara Hardy

When we make use of the crude, common, convenient term "world" in order to say something about the work of a novelist, we probably have in mind one or more of these meanings: the refraction of social and personal experience, from which we may inferentially reconstruct a source "world," rather as Humphry House does in *The Dickens World;* the uniquely typical life of the novel's imaginary and consistent history, geography, population, ethos, sociology, metaphysics; and the total *oeuvre* which bears the imprint of its novelist-god. We bring to the reponse and analysis of all or any of these worlds that private and public world which we ourselves inhabit, making our inferences and reconstructions according to our time, place, personal experience, belief and life-style. The world of George Eliot and the world of *Middlemarch* is remade for each reader and at each reading. As someone remarked at one of the three *Middlemarch* conferences in 1971–72, "Why did *we* write *these* papers?" The answers were too complex, private and inaccessible to be appended.

If as critics of fiction we take our bearings not only from each other but from what our novelist perceives about the nature of fiction, we find that George Eliot discourages us from using the term "world" unreflectively. One of the things *Middlemarch* has to show, explicitly and implicitly, is the plurality of personal worlds. We learn to handle the metaphor as a metaphor, provisionally and ironically, both when reading novels and when reflecting on those worlds outside novels which are made up of many kinds of experience, including that of reading novels.

From *Particularities: Readings in George Eliot.* © 1982 by Barbara Hardy. Peter Owen Ltd., 1982.

The word "world" occurs in *Middlemarch* in the final sentence, as late and as memorably as possible. By the time she gets there George Eliot has earned the right both to vagueness and to melioristic suggestion in words which could not be taken from a first sentence in any of her novels: "the growing good of the world is partly dependent on unhistoric acts." This open and extensive use of the word includes past and future, is morally and socially undefined, and derives meaning from everything that has come before it in the novel. The first use of "world" is a very closed, precise and relativist one, which makes it plain that George Eliot sees the individuality of such acts of construction. She tells us in chapter 1 that Dorothea's mind "was theoretic, and yearned by its nature after some lofty conception of the world which might frankly include the parish of Tipton and her own rule of conduct there." The imagery of yearning and height emphasises the activity of construction, Dorothea's characteristic range from near to far, her refusal to be either abstract or parochial, her beginning with self and Tipton, and her aspirations beyond into the larger "world."

The next emphatic appearance of the word comes when Casaubon introduces his "world" in chapter 2, at the dinner party in Tipton Grange where he and Dorothea first meet. His use of the word is in one sense large, but is essentially restricted both in time and personal style: "My mind is something like the ghost of an ancient, wandering about the world and trying mentally to construct it as it used to be, in spite of ruin and confusing changes." Dorothea immediately picks up and reinterprets his ideal of construction in the light of her own, judging and deprecating her loftiness in comparison with what seems to be the new Casaubon scale:

> To reconstruct a past world, doubtless with a view to the highest purposes of truth—what a work to be in any way present at, to assist in, though only as a lamp-holder!

The reconstruction continues in the next chapter, and after an evening, a day, and the part of a morning spent in his company, she concludes:

> "He thinks with me," said Dorothea to herself, "or rather, he thinks a whole world of which my thought is but a poor twopenny mirror. And his feelings too, his whole experience—what a lake compared with my little pool!"

After Casaubon drives off to Lowick at three o'clock on the "beautiful breezy autumn day," Dorothea walks in the wood, thinking intensely about her need for Casaubon as a guide to the past. Casaubon has been introduced to the reader as a historian, and George Eliot emphasises Dorothea's historical consciousness, her sense of the past, and its relation to her needs in the present, and for the future. Walking along the bridle path, she longs for a guide "who would take her along the grandest path." The literal and metaphorical imagery of paths insists that she has failed to read the significance of Casaubon's introductory images; all too accurately he describes himself as like a ghost—but of an ancient, capable only of "wandering . . . and trying" rather than firmly guiding. He is a historian who ignores the evidence of history, "trying mentally to construct it as it used to be, in spite of ruin and confusing changes." Compare Dorothea's very different sense of futurity:

> "There would be nothing trivial about our lives. Everyday-things with us would mean the greatest things. It would be like marrying Pascal. I should learn to see the truth by the same light as great men have seen it by. And then I should know what to do, when I got older: I should see how it was possible to lead a grand life here—now—in England."

> (chap. 3)

She inserts into her view of Casaubon's world view her own moral purpose of practical and immediate construction, and her emphasis on the here-and-now and England strongly contrasts with his backward, evidence-ignoring, time-leaping look, just as her careful but innocent gloss "doubtless for the highest purposes of truth" draws attention to his entire neglect of moral end. Perhaps the greatest contrast is between the intensity and vigour of her language, feelings and movement, and his total languor and flatness. The speech about the ghost of an ancient is a non-answer to Brooke's questions about Southey (Casaubon having pardonably failed in "keeping pace with Mr. Brooke's impetuous reason") and it is also expressively delivered, "with precision, as if he had been called upon to make a public statement" and in a "balanced sing-song neatness."

Casaubon's images for the historical sense are dead and unselfconsciously archaic, Dorothea's are alive and self-reflectively modern. Casaubon recognises the existence of change, and has after all written his "timely" pamphlet on the Catholic question; but he finds the evidence of historical change an obstacle to his static research as he tries to reconstruct the far past without taking account of the processes of history. Dorothea's viewpoint is not only self-reflectively modern, but very close to the most influential self-conscious reflections on the nature of history which were available to George Eliot, at the time of writing *Middlemarch* (1869–71) as

well as the time of the novel's action (1829 to 1831). Carlyle wrote two
essays in *Fraser's Magazine* (in 1830 and 1833) which insisted on the participation of the present in the consciousness of history and which described
history, in an image which needs no underlining, as "a web" composed of
unrecorded acts, as inclusive of the present, as including the moderns both
as actors and as relators. Here are two extracts from Carlyle's essay "On
History Again" (1833):

> Only he who understands what has been, can know what
> should be and will be. It is of the last importance that the indi-
> vidual have ascertained his relation to the whole; "an individual
> helps not," it has been written: "only he who unites with many
> at the proper hour." How easy, in a sense, for your well-in-
> structed Nanac [Nanac Shah too, we remember, steeped him-
> self three days in some sacred Well; and there learnt enough] to
> work without waste or force (or what we call fault); and, in
> practice, act new History, as perfectly as, in theory he knew the
> old! Comprehending what the given world was, and what it
> had and what it wanted, how might his clear effort strike-in at
> the right time and the right point; wholly increasing the true
> current and tendency, nowhere cancelling itself in opposition
> thereto! Unhappily, such smooth-running, ever-accelerated
> course is nowise the one appointed us.

> To use a ready-made similitude, we might liken Universal His-
> tory to a magic web; and consider with astonishment how, by
> philosophic insight and indolent neglect, the ever-growing fab-
> ric wove itself forward, out of that ravelled immeasurable mass
> of threads and thrums, which we name *Memoirs;* nay, at each
> new lengthening, at each new *epoch,* changed its whole propor-
> tions, its hue and structure to the very origin. Thus, do not the
> records of a Tacitus acquire new meaning, after seventeen hun-
> dred years, in the hands of a Montesquieu? Niebuhr has to rein-
> terpret for us, at a still greater distance, the writings of a Titus
> Livius: nay, the religious archaic chronicles of a Hebrew
> Prophet and Lawgiver escape not the like fortune; and many a
> ponderous Eichhorn scans, with new ground philosophic spec-
> tacles, the revelation of a Moses, and strives to reproduce for
> this century what, thirty centuries ago, was of plainly infinite
> significance to all. Consider History with the beginnings of it
> stretching dimly into the remote Time; emerging darkly out of

the mysterious Eternity: the ends of it enveloping *us* at this hour, whereof we at this hour, both as actors and relators, form part!

Middlemarch is the first English novel to analyse the psychology of historical consciousness. Its analysis involves seeing the relation of public and private worlds, recognising that private experience shapes the sense of the public, just at the "larger public life" shapes the private world.

In *The Historical Novel* Lukács is concerned with the ways in which novelists reflect and analyse historic events and historic causality. It is true, as he says, that the necessary condition for the growth of the historical novel was the development of historical and global consciousness at the beginning of the nineteenth century. It is also true, as he knew, that the new genre of historical novel led to sharper reflections on the historical consciousness which fed back again into the social novel, enriching its presentation of the private and public life. George Eliot provides us with an instance which falls outside the categories of Lukacs. *Middlemarch* is not only an instance of History by Indirection, as Jerome Beaty has shown, and an exploration of History as Analogy, as David Carroll argued soon after Beaty, but is a very precocious novel about the sense of history. It describes as a part of a psychological, moral and social complex, what it feels like to have and to use the sense of history. Dorothea knows that she relates to the immediate and distant past, she is fully conscious of the Carlylean continuity in which yesterday continues history into today, and in which tomorrow needs to be aware of last week, last year, and last century. This awareness is examined not only in Dorothea but throughout *Middlemarch*. It is shown in many variant forms, negative and positive. It is evaluated in presences, absences and displacements. Its analysis proffers one of the most original insights in *Middlemarch*.

The insight is highly characteristic of George Eliot, who as a novelist seems to have incorporated into her art most swiftly and subtly her creative experiences as well as those from life. Perhaps all great works of art are about themselves, and in order fully to see this self-preoccupation in *Middlemarch* we too have to look back into the history of her other novels. Into each novel goes what has been learnt from the previous ones, not only as the craft matures but as her experience as a novelist instructs her in the themes of imagination and narration. In and through writing she learnt more about imagination and love, about the ways in which we shape our sense of the world inside and outside novels. For instance, her interest in the life-narrations which loom large in all experience was fairly rudimentary in *Scenes of Clerical Life,* but it became a prominent aspect of fictional psychology in *Adam Bede* and *The Mill on the Floss,* which took their author's experience of storytelling into their content and argument, as well as into their form. One could say the same about her interest in imagistic and dramatic modes. Her experience of metaphor is incorporated in her handling of Casaubon's and Featherstone's imagination, in her analysis of the way their thinking gets entangled in metaphor, and her experience of the lyrical intensities and limits of poetry gets into the presentation of Ladislaw. The experience of studying and imagining the past, familiar to the author of all these retrospective novels, was of course most intense in the writing of *Romola,* her only conventional historical novel. But the other fiction is instructive too.

George Eliot's way of connecting outer and inner, public and private, historic and unhistoric, is to locate and understand the link within the individual consciousness. She does not historicise the life of the individual, perhaps having learnt from *Romola.* Nor does she dehistoricise experience by showing the gulf between the private and the public life as she did in *Scenes of Clerical Life,* where she stressed the historical colour, and emphasised the date of customs and costumes, while exclaiming about the past's innocence of its future, through sudden shifts of perspective in which characters and passions were highlighted against history. In "Mr. Gilfil's Love Story," for instance, the narrator makes a bid for pathos by switching from personal foreground to public background rather artificially, using the historical perspective to "mark the time" and to act as an intensifier of the heroine's small helplessness:

> While this poor little heart was being bruised with a weight too heavy for it, Nature was holding on her calm inexorable way, in unmoved and terrible beauty. The stars were rushing in their eternal courses; the tides swelled to the level of the last expectant weed; the sun was making brilliant day to busy nations on the other side of the swift earth. The stream of human thought and deed was hurrying and broadening onward. The astronomer was at his telescope; the great ships were labouring over the waves; the toiling eagerness of commerce, the fierce spirit of revolution, were only ebbing in brief rest; and sleepless statesmen were dreading the possible crisis of the morrow. What were our little Tina and her trouble in this mighty torrent, rushing from one awful unknown to another? Lighter than the smallest centre of quivering life in the water-drop, hidden and uncared for as the pulse of anguish in the breast of the

tiniest bird that has fluttered down to its nest with the long-sought food, and has found the next torn and empty.

(chap. 5)

This transition marks a parallel, instead of a contrast, between private and public passions:

> The last chapter has given the discerning reader sufficient insight into the state of things at Cheveral Manor in the summer of 1788. In that summer, we know, the great nation of France was agitated by conflicting thoughts and passions, which were but the beginnings of sorrows. And in our Caterina's little breast, too, there were terrible struggles.
>
> (chap. 3)

These are crude and arbitrary uses of historical reference, and although she was to continue to use history as background and analogy in *Daniel Deronda,* the image of historical perspective reappears there in a newly functional form, registering in portentous questions the sense of history inside Gwendolen's mind. George Eliot has several times remarked Gwendolen's lack of any historical sense by the comparison with the grand march of events, and at the end of the novel forces her to feel the powerful pressure of the public world:

> "What are you going to do?" she asked, at last, very timidly. "Can I understand the ideas, or am I too ignorant?"
>
> "I am going to the East to become better acquainted with the condition of my race in various countries there," said Deronda, gently—anxious to be as explanatory as he could on what was the impersonal part of their separateness from each other. "The idea that I am possessed with is that of restoring a political existence to my people, making them a nation again, giving them a national centre, such as the English have, though they too are scattered over the face of the globe. That is a task which presents itself to me as a duty: I am resolved to begin it, however feebly. I am resolved to devote my life to it. At the least, I may awaken a movement in other minds, such as has been awakened in my own."
>
> There was a long silence between them. The world seemed getting larger round poor Gwendolen, and she more solitary and helpless in the midst. The thought that he might come back after going to the East, sank before the bewildering vision

of these wide-stretching purposes in which she felt herself reduced to a mere speck. There comes a terrible moment to many souls when the great movements of the world, the larger destinies of mankind, which have lain aloof in newspapers and other neglected reading, enter like an earthquake into their own lives—when the slow urgency of growing generations turns into the tread of an invading army or the dire clash of civil war, and grey fathers know nothing to seek for but the corpses of their blooming sons, and girls forget all vanity to make lint and bandages which may serve for the shattered limbs of their betrothed husbands.

It is the experience of writing *Middlemarch* which has transformed the image. There is some sense now in making a to-do about the gap between the public and the private event and passion, because the novelist has come to see the moral implications of wondering and caring about the great world. The characters in *Scenes of Clerical Life* and *Adam Bede* were innocents. Maggie Tulliver asked many questions about the nature, use and relevance of logic, literature, and geometry, but the acknowledgment of her historical identity is made by the author's commentary, outside the character. We see that Maggie is representative of certain restrictions and limitations, in sex, family, occupation, society, and ethos, but we also see her ignorance of the historical conditions. *Romola* is a historical novel, which reconstructs major events and historical characters and also attempts, in Thackerayan fashion, to show the quotidian and familiar inhabitants of a past time. The effort to imagine and to research for *Romola* must have made George Eliot sharply conscious of the historian's activity and may have led her, in *Middlemarch,* to put the historical action inside the mind; this psychological analysis of historical thinking was probably helped also by the writing of *Felix Holt,* a more external novel about the 1832 Reform Act which left her freer to explore what Carlyle saw as the historical significance of the unhistoric life. *Felix Holt* exhausted the desire to show political reaction and characters, and she was free in *Middlemarch* to locate the consciousness of history within her characters. But *Romola* provided the crucial experience, for in writing it she had to think about the relation of cultural and social history, the nature of historical consciousness, and the purpose and reception of a novel written for the present age about the past. Perhaps the greatest achievement of *Romola* was to make *Middlemarch* possible.

Middlemarch is a novel about good and bad historians. It is also about people, good and bad, who have no sense of history. In *Daniel Deronda*

George Eliot is writing from the moral base delicately but firmly created by Jane Austen in *Mansfield Park,* where she relates Fanny Price's awareness of the larger world—"Did you not hear me question him about the slave-trade?"—to her capacity for rhapsody, wonder, veneration, sympathy, and knowledge. In *Daniel Deronda,* as in *Mansfield Park,* virtue is forced out of its fugitive cloisters into a sense of the world, but in *Middlemarch* George Eliot shows a realistic tolerance of decent people without much sense of history. Less like a fable than any of her other novels, *Middlemarch* has a moral spectrum of many shades. History is projected indirectly, as Jerome Beaty has said, sometimes off-centre, sometimes muted, sometimes statically but vividly imaged, as in Rome, the city of visible history. George Eliot's concern with the historical consciousness in *Middlemarch* is not simply a moral one, for she observes the coexistence of a public sense with moral responsibility or moral inactivity, and the coexistence of public ignorance with a lack of moral sense or with moral decency.

Rosamond Vincy has no historical sense, and rests unperturbed, while her father, whose historical sense is strong in those connections and causes that affect his trade, tells her with bluntness that she wasn't educated to marry a poor man and that this is a bad time to do so, "with this disappointment about Fred, and Parliament going to be dissolved, and machine-breaking everywhere, and an election coming":

> "Dear papa! what can that have to do with my marriage?"
>
> "A pretty deal to do with it! We may all be ruined for what I know—the country's in that state! Some say it's the end of the world, and be hanged if I don't think it looks like it. Anyhow, it's not a time for me to be drawing money out of my business, and I should wish Lydgate to know that."
>
> "I'm sure he expects nothing, papa. And he has such very high connections: he is sure to rise in one way or another. He is engaged in making scientific discoveries."
>
> (chap. 36)

Vincy's sense of the world is worldy-wise, Rosamond's worldly and ignorant, insufficient for an appraisal of her lot, frighteningly sufficient for persuasion. She silences her father by a superficially impressive mention of "scientific discoveries," and he cuts no ice with his quick run-through of topical disasters, private and public. Their dialogue makes no simple correlation of virtue and knowledge; Vincy's narrow sense of the larger world is created and bounded by self-interest, innocent both of scientific discoveries and their possible relation to "rising in one way or another." (The last phrase is a tiny example of George Eliot's apparently effortless wringing of irony from the common phrase.) Rosamond runs randomly through various facts about Lydgate, "See how he has been called in by the Chettams and Casaubons"; "And he has such very high connections: he is sure to rise in one way or another. He is engaged in making scientific discoveries"; "Mr. Lydgate is a gentleman." Her sense of social causality is dangerously obtuse; these two materialists, father and daughter, the warmhearted and the cold, have a worldly sense but no imaginative knowledge of the public world.

There is a famous instance of displacement quoted by Gordon Haight and Jerome Beaty, when at the end of the novel various Middlemarch Tories are gathered together at Freshitt Hall, in October 1831, discussing the defeat of the Reform Bill. Because of the Bill "Mr. Cadwallader came to be walking on the slope of the lawn near the great conservatory at Freshitt Hall, holding the 'Times' in his hands behind him, while he talked with a trout-fisher's dispassionateness about the prospects of the country to Sir James Chettam." Not only the men but "the ladies talked politics, though more fitfully." From this fitful feminine talk the political facts filter through. Gossip is sifted through the response of various private passions and humours: Mrs. Cadwallader, representing birth and breeding, "was strong on the intended creation of peers" which she has learnt about from her aristocratic cousin; Lady Chettam is dim, decorous and irrelevant, Celia dotingly maternal, "It would be very nice, though, if he were a Viscount." When Mr. Brooke arrives the others naturally interpret his gloom as political, only to find that it is his response to Dorothea's intended marriage and not to the Lords' rejection of the Bill. So the personal event immediately takes over from the crisis in the public world, not only for Brooke, but for the whole party. George Eliot is displacing history not simply to present it with subtlety but to insist that private relationships and interest drive out the larger happening.

One of her most interesting scenes of displacement comes in chapter 56, where the public world is elaborately and prominently analysed. It opens quietly, marking the connection between the construction of the railways and Caleb Garth's newly undertaken management of the farms and tenements attached to Lowick Manor. Although George Eliot insists that in praising Dorothea's "head for business," Caleb had in mind not money but the skilful application of labour, he is plainly said to have "a bias towards getting the best possible terms from railway companies." He undertakes a survey with the railway's agents, and it is interrupted by "six or seven" labourers attacking with their hayforks. George Eliot has more elaborate treatment of historical events in this chapter than anywhere else in the novel, and its displacement is the more pointed. The introductory exposition is built up with careful attention to steps and stages, in a long, witty, dramatised exposition on the views of the women who swear that nothing will bring them to travel by rail, and the proprietors who intend to get the highest possible price "for permission to injure mankind." The slow understanding of Solomon Featherstone, the road overseer, is then unfolded for comedy and social representation. He isn't exactly a fool: "Well, there's this to be said, Jane . . . the more spokes we put in their wheel the more they'll pay us to let 'em go on, if they must come whether or not." There follows the careful analysis of Solomon's by no means un-subtle and ineffective provocations, and the revolt of the Frick labourers, bored, suspicious, conservative, anti-urban, and all for a bit of "good foon." In spite of its rather condescending humour about the rustic rebels, this scene is one in which George Eliot raises a central political question, one which she finds and leaves unanswerable. "Nettle-seed needs no dig-ging," but the one labourer who stands outside the attack, old Timothy Cooper, "who had stayed behind turning his hay while the others had been gone on their spree," with the full authority of intelligence, experi-ence, and nonviolence, accuses Caleb Garth of being exactly what he is, a master's man. Caleb has been speaking soothingly, his author approving of his artless pauses and images:

> "But come, you didn't mean any harm. Somebody told you the railroad was a bad thing. That was a lie. It may do a bit of harm here and there, to this and to that; and so does the sun in heaven. But the railway's a good thing."
>
> "Aw! good for the big folks to make money out on," said old Timothy Cooper, who had stayed behind turning his hay while the others had been gone on their spree;—"I'n seen lots o' things turn up sin' I war a young un—the war an' the peace, and the canells, an' the oald King George, an' the Regen', an' the new King George, an' the new un as has got a new ne-ame—an' its been all aloike to the poor mon. What's the canells been t'him? They'n brought him neyther me-at nor be-acon, nor wage to lay by, if he didn't save it wi' clemmin' his own inside. Times ha' got wusser for him sin' I war a young un. An' so it'll be wi' the railroads. They'll on'y leave the poor mon furder behind. But them are fools as meddle, and so I told the chaps here. This is the big folks's world, this is. But yo're for the big folks, Muster Garth, yo are."

It is a powerful moment, and rises to an even higher peak when George Eliot has the sense and candour to admit not only that Caleb has no reply, but that there is no reply:

> Timothy was a wiry old labourer, of a type lingering in those times—who had his savings in a stocking-foot, lived in a lone cottage, and was not to be wrought on by any oratory, having as little of the feudal spirit, and believing as little, as if he had not been totally unacquainted with the Age of Reason and the Rights of Man. Caleb was in a difficulty known to any person attempting in dark times and unassisted by miracle to reason with rustics who are in possession of an undeniable truth which they know through a hard process of feeling, and can let it fall like a giant's club on your neatly-carved argument for a social benefit which they do *not* feel.

Timothy completes the drama and shatters the argument, and his role and function are specially satisfying when one compares him with Dickens's Stephen Blackpool: Timothy's wise and consistent detachment does not criticise his fellow-labourers, but speaks from his hay-turning, and to the point. The scene is thorough in analysis and self-contained in drama, depending on striking nonce-characters and real political debate. All the more startling, then, to find this political impact abruptly displaced. For the coming of the railway is not there in its own right but is used instrumentally to discover Fred Vincy's moment of vocation. What was shown as a vital and unresolved clash between socially representative forces comes to be described as an accident:

> For the effective accident is but the touch of fire where there is oil and tow; and it always appeared to Fred that the railway brought the needed touch.

Fred is not lowered by his self-interest and lack of social imagination, but George Eliot seems to bring her own social imagination into unusually full play, in order most calmly to turn its direction. What had seemed of central interest was not, after all, the point of the scene, and the large historical events of the railway and revolt recede in interest, like a Holy Family inconspicuous in a corner of a Breugel, and truly enough, since for Caleb and Fred the personal life is what matters. It is a crisis of some social moment in the personal life, too, but the sense of a diversion from history is still impressive. For Caleb and Fred the railway was only the precipitating accident, and when Caleb tells his wife the story of the day George Eliot repeats the displacement by devoting a mere summarising half-sentence to the labourers' attack, and over a page to the personal crisis: "He had already narrated the adventure which had brought about Fred's sharing in his work, but had kept back the further result." In the story of love, vocation, and parenthood, the historical moment is subordinate, so it is foreshortened, diminished and dismissed.

Here George Eliot has her history and reduces it to the appropriate proportions, as she may have learnt to do from *Romola,* where she had not managed things quite so well. It was her 1829, and it was her reader's 1829, from their perspective of 1871–72; but for Caleb and Fred it was the innocent present tense, and the historical significance of their date and their adventure lay in the future.

For Dorothea, the present is not historically innocent. To go back to the beginning, in that first big social scene in chapter 2, where Casaubon and Chettam dine with Brooke and his two nieces in a promisingly mixed and unmarried party, the characters present the public world through private passions, tastes and concerns. The historical sense is dramatised as an interest naturally, waywardly, and unpredictably correlated with conscience. Like Jane Austen in *Mansfield Park,* George Eliot is writing about social conscience and social consciousness, and the dinner party acts like many of Jane Austen's group scenes to show the snatch-and-grab action of social converse, and the personal impetus behind our sense of the public world. We make up our private and public worlds at the same time, and the relation between the two is complex. Chapter 2 establishes time, place and culture in a desultory but continuous conversation, its slivers of talk brilliantly suiting the small dinner party of intimates, acquaintances and strangers. The talk turns round, and each turn is public in theme, private in motive and address. The chapter-motto is Don Quixote's transformation of the basin into the Helmet of Mambrino, the emblem standing for Dorothea's aspiration, nobility, madness, delusion, anachronism and appositely prefacing a scene of multiple illusion where the characters clandestinely and mistakenly solicit each other. Brooke soliloquises erratically, fixed by one of George Eliot's sharp alliterative shafts, as "these motes from the mass of a magistrate's mind" shame Dorothea, conscious chiefly of the Locke-like Casaubon; Chettam, "excellent baronet," hopefully woos Dorothea with Davy's Agricultural Chemistry; Casaubon is alerted by Dorothea's energetic and high-principled speech; Dorothea is entangled by modest self-abnegatory boasts; Celia finds Casaubon's moles repugnant and pities Sir James's delusions; Casaubon makes his revealing speech about living with the dead. The public world is rapidly sketched in this private drama, where the counters are Wordsworth, Humphrey Davy, Cambridge, agricultural experiments, electricity, Adam Smith, political economy, the limitations of young ladies, Southey, hunting, rural housing, and Wilberforce. As the hard facts of history are blown about like bubbles, the public is there for the readers because it is there for the characters. George Eliot fixes the ways in which people create their fictions of each other, shows how the private fiction merges with the public, and begins to measure the weight of the individual public consciences.

The novel distinguishes two dimensions, the public and the personal, or the historic and the unhistoric. It was not wrong for Fred and Caleb to fail to observe how their personal interests were minor events, compared with the coming of the railway or Timothy's unanswerable argument. But for Mr. Brooke, philanthropist and would-be politician, or Casaubon, cleric and would-be historian, there is a moral failure. What they attempt is life in the public world, so their failures in public consciousness *are* failures. It is as a religious historian that Casaubon is first introduced, and it is as a historian that he first speaks of himself. What he says is highly significant, and we are required not only to attend to the words but also to Dorothea's swift quixotic interpretation:

> "I feed too much on the inward sources; I live too much with the dead. My mind is something like the ghost of an ancient, wandering about the world and trying mentally to construct it as it used to be, in spite of ruin and confusing changes."

Romola too contains the ghost of an ancient, and in it George Eliot learnt the difficulties and sterilities of trying to reconstruct a past world, of going back, like Casaubon, over irksome intervening timemarks. Casaubon's researches were shaped by his author's, and in her presentation of his historical scholarship, the debt to *Romola* is almost too painfully plain. Sartre's Roquentin gave up history for fiction because history lacked particulars; Casaubon is certainly the kind of historian who lacks a sense of particulars as he also lacks Carlyle's sense that history must include the present. Casaubon as historian is doubly dead, not only the ghost but the ghost of an ancient, and one who tried to reconstruct the past "in spite of ruin and confusing changes" as if process could be ignored. Casaubon is the negation of the historical consciousness, and Dorothea (Fanny Price's successor) is its active exemplar. Her concern is conspicuously aware of the present, and she is unable to ignore ruin and confusing changes. She is not the only character in search of historical meaning, but the most urgent and ingenuous seeker. When we first see her she interprets Casaubon's too revealing self-description according to her own needs to reconstruct her past for an epistemological purpose: "To reconstruct a past world, doubtless with a view to the highest purposes of truth—what a work to be in any way present at, to assist in, though only as a lampholder!" The highest purposes of truth are vague, but George Eliot's point about Dorothea's meliorism (perhaps about religion in general) is that it is vague, admiring glorious things in a blind sort of way, as Dorothea tells Will, widening the skirts of light. Still, there is precision as well as vagueness in Dorothea's inner narrative and as she revises her vision, in that fluent reworking of memory and fantasy which composes consciousness, she becomes decidedly less vague. She wants to reconstruct the past in order to know how to live in the present: "The thing which seemed to her best, she wanted to justify by the completest knowledge; and not to live in a pretended admission of rules which were never acted on." This becomes more concrete as her fantasy of instructive marriage weaves its web:

> There would be nothing trivial about our lives. Everyday-things with us would mean the greatest things. It would be like marrying Pascal. I should learn to see the truth by the same light as great men have seen it by. And then I should know what to do, when I got older: I should see how it was possible to lead a grand life here—now—in England.
>
> (chap. 3)

It seems possible that T. S. Eliot, who admired George Eliot, may have found his namesake's words echoing somewhere in the mind when in *Little Gidding,* also concerned with pressures of past on the present and needs for tradition, he wrote, "Now and in England," and "History is now and England." Dorothea's need for history is not unlike T. S. Eliot's.

She is badly in need of the "guide who would take her along the grandest path" when she goes from England on her wedding journey to Rome. We first see her there, usefully and appropriately, through the eyes of two other historians, Naumann and Will Ladislaw. Naumann is a key figure, who as a Nazarene painter has his own interest in going back in time. He calls Will to come and admire his "fine bit of antitheseis."

> "There lies antique beauty, not corpse-like even in death, but arrested in the complete contentment of its sensuous perfection: and here stands beauty in its breathing life, with the consciousness of Christian centuries in its bosom."
>
> (chap. 19)

and a little later:

> "If you were an artist, you would think of Mistress Second-Cousin as antique form animated by Christian sentiment—a sort of Christian Antigone—sensuous force controlled by spiritual passion."
>
> (chap. 19)

Will explains the theory that lies behind this conscious interest in historical compression through symbol, when he tells Casaubon later on that his friend is one "of the chief renovators of Christian art, one of those who had not only revived but expanded that grand conception of supreme events as mysteries at which the successive ages were spectators, and in relation to which the great souls of all periods became as it were contemporaries" (chap. 22). He dazzlingly flatters Casaubon and amuses Dorothea by the account of his mimicry of Naumann's "breadth of intention" by painting Tamburlaine in his chariot representing "the tremendous course of the world's physical history lashing on the harnessed dynasties." Dorothea, a little less humourless than she has been made out, sees the joke:

> "Do you intend Tamburlaine to represent earthquakes and volcanoes?"
>
> "O yes," said Will, laughing, "and migrations of races and clearings of forests—and America and the steam-engine. Everything you can imagine!"
>
> "What a difficult kind of shorthand!" said Dorothea, smiling towards her husband. "It would require all your knowledge to be able to read it."

George Eliot's conversational small-change can be as resonant as her imagery: "everything you can imagine" and "it would require all your knowledge" are to reveal their density: to understand the course of the world's history indeed requires everything that Dorothea can imagine and more than all Casaubon's knowledge.

Her imagination does rather better than his knowledge, when she asks him about another mythical picture, Raphael's *Cupid and Psyche,* Dorothea asks a personal and passionate question, about personal feeling, "But do you care about them?" when he has impersonally and coldly commended the frescoes because "most persons think it worthwhile" to visit them. He turns away Dorothea's "But do you care" to reply in the passive voice, "They are, I believe, highly esteemed," and speaks from a pedant's knowledge and judgment, having nothing else:

"They are, I believe, highly esteemed. Some of them represent the fable of Cupid and Psyche, which is probably the romantic invention of a literary period, and cannot, I think, be reckoned as a genuine mythical product. But if you like these wall-paintings we can easily drive thither; and you will then, I think, have seen the chief works of Raphael, any of which it were a pity to omit in a visit to Rome. He is the painter who has been held to combine the most complete grace of form with sublimity of expression. Such at least I have gathered to be the opinion of cognoscenti."

This kind of answer given in a measured official tone, as of a clergyman reading according to the rubric, did not help to justify the glories of the Eternal City, or to give her the hope that if she knew more about them the world would be joyously illuminated for her.

(chap. 20)

Sexual passion, nerve, beauty, light, loss—he is blind to these, even on his wedding journey in Rome. His is the dulled scholar's inability to speak personally, passionately, even aesthetically to the eager student of culture who demands personal response, but finds only arid scholarship, and conventional judgment.

Dorothea is also attempting a personal response to Rome's bewildering cultural mixture which confounds her by its sensuality, its aestheticism, and its "ruin and confusing changes." It is perfectly in keeping with Casaubon's lack of passion that he should fail to respond to *Cupid and Psyche* and to the Romantic period, but equally important and less conspicuous is the total failure of his historical sense. The demand that he should relate past to present is implicit in her "do you care?" What Naumann so confidently sees and renders in visual symbols of Christian art, through an ethical aesthetic mediaevalism that can condense, assimilate, and reconstruct, and what Will so brilliantly parodies in his claim that Rome's very miscellaneousness "made the mind flexible with constant comparison, and saved you from seeing the world's ages as a set of box-like partitions without vital connection," is precisely the complex record of history and culture that startles and troubles Dorothea. It is no simple case of culture-shock; her struggles in England are also struggles to understand the environment, to relate the manor house and the tenant's pig-sty cottage, the politics and neglected fences, the smirking Correggiosities in Tipton Manor and the poverty outside, theory and practice, art and nature. Rome, where Dorothea's strength is low, and her susceptibility strained, is not only a superb symbol of the history of politics, religion and art but a correlative for the shocks and revulsions of the wedding journey:

After the brief narrow experience of her girlhood she was beholding Rome, the city of visible history, where the past of a whole hemisphere seems moving in funeral procession with strange ancestral images and trophies gathered from afar.

But this stupendous fragmentariness heightened the dreamlike strangeness of her bridal life. Dorothea had now been five weeks in Rome, and in the kindly mornings when autumn and winter seemed to go hand in hand like a happy aged couple one of whom would presently survive in chiller loneliness, she had driven about at first with Mr. Casaubon, but of late chiefly with Tantripp and their experienced courier. She had been led through the best galleries, had been taken to the chief points of view, had been shown the greatest ruins and the most glorious churches, and she had ended by oftenest choosing to drive out to the Campagna where she could feel alone with the earth and sky, away from the oppressive masquerade of ages, in which her own life too seemed to become a masque with enigmatical costumes.

To those who have looked at Rome with the quickening power of a knowledge which breathes a growing soul into all historic shapes, and traces out the suppressed transitions which unite all contrasts, Rome may still be the spiritual centre and interpreter of the world. But let them conceive one more historical contrast: the gigantic broken revelations of that Imperial and Papal city thrust abruptly on the notions of a girl who had been brought up in English and Swiss Puritanism, fed on meagre Protestant histories and on art chiefly of the hand-screen sort; a girl whose ardent nature turned all her small allowance of knowledge into principles, fusing her actions into their mould, and whose quick emotions gave the most abstract things the quality of a pleasure or a pain; a girl who had lately become a wife, and from the enthusiastic acceptance of untried duty found herself plunged in tumultuous preoccupation with her personal lot. The weight of unintelligible Rome might lie easily on bright nymphs to whom it formed a background for the brilliant picnic of Anglo-foreign society; but Dorothea had no such defence against deep impressions. Ruins and basilicas, palaces and colossi, set in the midst of a sordid present, where all that was living and warm-blooded seemed sunk in the deep degeneracy of a superstition divorced from reverence; the dimmer but yet eager Titanic life gazing and struggling on walls and ceilings; the long vistas of white forms whose marble eyes seemed to hold the monotonous light of an alien world: all this vast wreck of ambitious ideals, sensuous and spiritual, mixed confusedly with the signs of breathing forgetfulness and degradation, at first jarred her as with an electric shock, and then urged themselves on her with that ache belonging to a glut of confused ideas which check the flow of emotion.

(chap. 20)

Dorothea's sense of history does not make sense of Rome. The debate with Will is broken off by Casaubon's illness and never taken up again during the novel; for Will ceases to represent Shelleyan Romanticism and Nazarene discipleship, and moves into politics. He retains his ability to make connections as we see when he rebukes Brooke for trying to box off his philanthropy from Reform. Dorothea never receives the answer about the present from the past, but George Eliot sees, from the perspective of forty years later, what Dorothea needed to question in 1829.

Dorothea hasn't enough money to drain her piece of land and found her ideal community; she is far too late to be a Saint Theresa; she cannot even internalise her author's sharply feminist consciousness. Ideas about reform, vocation, culture, money, marriage, religion, meliorism, are all generalised and also internalised, refracted through the consciousness of Dorothea and others. Dorothea asks questions about history, not the young ladies' "toybox" history of the world which she was taught in that education "at once narrow and promiscuous," but a history which she both exemplifies and demands, a history that will make the past relevant to the present "here—now—in England." It is also a demand for a history which makes sense to an ordinary woman.

Ordinary in achievement but not in endowment, because she is endowed with George Eliot's historical imagination which tries to extend its personal experience through a knowledge of the public world, as truthfully and as feelingly as possible. Dorothea's strength lies in aspiration, not in action or creation. To call her creative efforts attempts at loving, like those of Little Dorrit, will not quite do, because her search is for culture, history, and economic information which she can use and relate to herself, her immediate environment, and her present. Dorothea asks for knowledge to be relevant, a hundred years before the demand created the household word, and her questioning is in the most radical spirit of challenge:

To poor Dorothea these severe classical nudities and smirking Renaissance–Correggiosities were painfully inexplicable, staring into the midst of her Puritanic conceptions: she had never been taught how she could bring them into any sort of relevance with her life.

(chap. 9)

If the novel's last sentence speaks of the unhistoric act, its first sentence speaks of history, in the largest sense of "the history of man." On several occasions George Eliot, quoting Fielding as a revered precedent, speaks of herself as a historian: she is writing the kind of novel which is not only better history than the conventional historical novel, but better history than is written by some historians. The novelist, unlike the historian, can create the innumerable biographies of individuals, and set her action in a remote valley, or a remote provincial society. Carlyle's first *Essay on History* (1830) is not only contemporaneous with the action of *Middlemarch,* but gives a fair picture of its mode of history:

Social Life is the aggregate of all the individual men's Lives who constitute society: History is the essence of innumerable Biographies. But if one Biography, nay our own Biography, study and recapitulate it as we may, remains in so many points unintelligible to us; how much more must these millions, the very facts of which, to say nothing of the purport of them, we know not, and cannot know!

and also:

Of the Historian himself, moreover, in his own special department, new and higher things are beginning to be expected. From of old, it was too often to be reproachfully observed of him, that he dwelt with disproportionate fondness in Senate-houses, in Battle-fields, nay, even in Kings' Antechambers; forgetting, that far away from such scenes, the mighty tide of Thought and Action was still rolling on its wondrous course, in gloom and brightness; and in its thousand remote valleys, a whole world of Existence, with or without an earthly sun of Happiness to warm it, with or without a heavenly sun of Holiness to purify and sanctify it, was blossoming and fading, whether the "famous victory" were won or lost.

George Eliot's novel illustrates and explains Carlyle, creating a kind of historical fiction not to be found in Lukács. The innumerable biographies make up history; the novelist can show not only the social and political pressures on ordinary lives, but also the pressures on remarkable people held back from remarkable achievements, denied biographers, having led only very private lives, resting "in unvisited tombs." An essential part of this portrayal of frustration and aspiration (in others beside Dorothea) is the action of historical consciousness. It is the convincing medium of quest and confusion, as well as the internalised version of the novel's own feat. In such ways *Middlemarch* earns its right to be vague in its last sentence, after so much precision and particularity:

The growing good of the world is partly dependent on unhistoric acts.

If *Middlemarch* is the most remarkable example before *Ulysses* of a novel about past and present, it is partly so by virtue of a consciousness of history which is shared by its heroine and its author. The consciousness led Dorothea to her unhistoric acts, but led George Eliot (whose tomb *is* visited) to the historic act of writing *Middlemarch*.

Middlemarch and the Woman Question

Kathleen Blake

Everybody says that *Middlemarch* is a great work. Many of its original re-viewers said that it raised the Woman Question. Yet the body of criticism from then till now makes surprisingly little case for it as a great feminist work. I think it is.

There are several ways of saying that *Middlemarch* is not a feminist novel. One is by arguing from one's own sexual stereotypes. In 1873 Fred-erick Napier Broome said that *Middlemarch* was not after all "some special impeachment of the fitness of the present female lot" because Dorothea did not represent a female character at all; Broome said she was a mascu-line type, since "unsatisfied ambitions are masculine rather than female ills." In 1974 John Halperin said that an epic life is not possible to Doro-thea—it is typical of one cast of modern sensibility to acquiesce in limita-tions that George Eliot asks us to feel as painful pressure. He goes on to say that Dorothea is not the epic type anyway. The only reason offered for this is her sex: "What she really needs as an object of devotion is a genuine husband and a family." This is "her discovery of her own nature and her real needs as a woman and a wife." Another recent critic, Bert Hornback, also reconciles himself cheerfully to Dorothea's fate. However doubtful a prize Will Ladislaw may be, "he is, however, real and male, a husband for Dorothea and a father for her child." Once accustomed to this point of view, we are not surprised—this is Halperin again—to hear Doro-thea compared to Amelia Smedley and George Eliot called "no feminist."

From *Nineteenth-Century Fiction* 31, no. 3 (December 1976). © 1976 by the Regents of the University of California.

Another way to divest *Middlemarch* of its feminism is to ignore the issue of sex altogether. A good example is found in an essay by Von Norbert Kohl treating the prelude as a guide to the novel. The prelude devotes much of its third paragraph (and there are only three) to a discussion of the "inconvenient indefiniteness" of "the natures of women." The paragraph offers several possible explanations for this phenomenon, but wherever one might decide that Eliot takes her stand on the issue, she has certainly posed it. However, what she poses, Kohl transposes. For woman's nature he substitutes human nature and discusses that.

A third argument against feminist interpretation of the book deserves to be taken more seriously. A number of nineteenth-century reviewers questioned whether the finale's indictment of society for its treatment of women is convincingly supported by the novel's action. Specifically, the first edition of 1871–72 says that Dorothea's mistakes owe something to a society that "smiled on propositions of marriage from a sickly man to a girl less than half his own age." The reviewers pointed out that Middlemarch did not smile, certainly not Celia, Mrs. Cadwallader, Sir James Chettam, not even Mr. Brooke. In 1873 Sidney Colvin offered a good response to this criticism, that Dorothea's whole education prepares her for the mistake of her marriage. However, Eliot did change the disputed paragraph. Specific criticism of social pressure towards marriage and of scanty education for women gives way in the 1874 edition, now taken as the standard, to a general complaint against "the conditions of an imperfect social state," which does not mention women at all. Is Eliot backing off from the Woman Question?

We know that she shared some of the feminist views of her period. In 1855 she wrote a sympathetic essay on Margaret Fuller and Mary Wollstonecraft that anticipates the concerns she takes up in *Middlemarch*: women's natures, their need for work, men's presumption of superiority and its destructive consequences. Eliot says of Fuller, "some of the best things she says are on the folly of absolute definitions of woman's nature and absolute demarcations of woman's mission." She quotes Fuller: "I think women need, especially at this juncture, a much greater range of occupation than they have, to rouse their latent powers" if they are to avoid "the *ennui* that haunts grown women." Both Wollstonecraft and Fuller write forcibly, says Eliot, on "the fact, that, while men have a horror of such faculty or culture in the other sex as tends to place it on a level with their own, they are really in a state of subjection to ignorant and feeble-minded women."

Still, avowedly feminist critics of *Middlemarch*—their number is small

considering the attention originally paid to the issue—tend to find their ex-
pectant feminism disappointed by the novel. I will return to this fourth
way of disqualifying *Middlemarch* as a feminist novel and argue against it
at the end of the essay. Now I wish to argue that the deletion of the indict-
ments of the finale makes little difference to the novel's focus on the disa-
bilities of a woman's lot.

The story begins and ends with Dorothea. Even in its revised state
the finale still completes the theme launched in the prelude. That theme
concerns what may be called the "Saint Theresa syndrome," the state of a
soul that aspires to epic life but finds no channel for "far-resonant action,"
and so achieves only a blundering life, its aspirations "dispersed among
hindrances." This fate is specifically feminine. The prelude concerns itself
with "the natures of women." The ardor that appears extravagant because
its object is so vague alternates with the "common yearning of womanhood." If she tries to take her stand anywhere but at the level that defines
her by sex—which Eliot hardly recommends, calling it a "lapse"—a woman's character becomes liable to the odd condition of "indefiniteness."

George Eliot is fascinated by this condition, as much of *Middlemarch*
goes to show. It may afflict men as well as women, but she repeats the
idea twice in the prelude in relation to women. The reason is that she is
not with those who judge that an "inconvenient indefiniteness" is part of
the fashioning of feminine nature by supreme power, for this psychic
slackness resists the scientific measurement that should be possible if it
were a natural given. Rather it is the result of social conditions, those
which favored Saint Theresa but do not favor Dorothea. It is interesting
that Eliot pictures a Saint Theresa not of mystic beatitude but of very concrete accomplishment, the reform of a religious order. To be favored is
to be able to "shape . . . thought and deed in noble agreement." But no
"coherent social faith and order" give latter-born Theresas something to
work for, and the result is "inconsistency and formlessness."

Women are especially vulnerable because society offers them so little
to do, expects less, and never imagines that they need work as much as
men do. A woman's life offers a paradigm of the novel's theme—lack of
vocation as tenuousness of identity. This may be why Eliot says that she,
like Herodotus, thinks it well to take a woman's lot as her starting point.
If she modified her finishing point to make it less specifically concerned
with the problems society creates for women, the modification is minor.
For there remain in the finale strong reminders of the social conditions that
break the force of women's strivings. In the water-obstruction imagery,
which is important in the novel and with which it ends, a full nature like

Dorothea's "spent itself in channels which had no great name on the earth."

Letty Garth, "whose life was much checkered by resistance to her depreciation as a girl," finds herself beleaguered in the finale by brotherly arguments and parental oracle that girls are good for less than boys. Letty seems to exist in *Middlemarch* so that the feminist theme may be simply stated now and again, lest it should be muffled in the massive orchestration. She is Middlemarch's staunchest feminist, "her feeling of superiority being stronger than her muscles." But Letty is only a little girl. It is doubtful that her feeling of superiority could last in a society that gives no credit to women even when it is due, let alone expects anything of them so that they might have something to aim at and to be. We learn in the finale that Middlemarch attributes Fred Vincy's book on farming to Mary because it is sure that he is above turnips and mangelwurzel. It attributes her book, drawn from Plutarch, to Fred because it is sure that whatever is the higher accomplishment must be his. In a society where even the disarming Mr. Brooke assumes that female intelligence "runs underground, like the rivers of Greece," to come out in the sons, and the amiable Sir James assumes that his masculine mind is of a higher kind than a woman's, no matter how soaring, as a birch to a palm tree, it is no surprise that Mary is not sorry to bring forth men children only. In his estimate of the soundness of ignorance itself if it is masculine, Sir James receives the benefit of tradition, which "furnishes the limpest personality with a little gum or starch." No such tradition holds female character together—hence its greater susceptibility to formlessness. We see what tradition Letty inherits.

George Eliot may have been right to modify the passage in the finale that blames Middlemarch for smiling on Dorothea's marriage to Casaubon, because the social pressures she actually shows are a good deal less direct, while none the less telling. Let us look at one instance among many that could be given of the subtle means by which Middlemarch delivers Dorothea into the arms of Casaubon. That it does not mean to only gives Eliot's analysis greater depth by avoiding the sentimentality of attributing every victim to somebody's intention.

Dorothea is characterized by ardor and energy. These words are used over and over to describe her. In chapter 1 she is "animated," has "inward fire," responds to a "current of feeling," "glowed." Her pleasure in the jewels and in riding establishes one component of her "Puritan energy," while her pleasure in renouncing them establishes the other. Dorothea enjoys her authority in her uncle's household, she has established an infant school in the village, she wants to arrange Mr. Brooke's papers, and she works on designs for cottages. She looks forward to the day when she will be of age to command her own money and implement her own schemes.

"Her mind was theoretic, and yearned by its nature after some lofty conception of the world which might frankly include the parish of Tipton." Several critics have misread Dorothea's character to conclude that there is something blamably abstract in her way of thinking, that her myopia symbolizes her oversight of the tangible in favor of nebulous ideals. While she often does not see what is before her face, and this can give her apprehension a certain Dodo quality, not all she overlooks is worth seeing—the Maltese puppy, for instance. Sometimes she is protected by her own blindness—"her blindness to whatever did not lie in her own pure purpose carried her safely by the side of precipices where vision would have been perilous with fear." Her idealizing vision is sometimes truer than the short view—her belief in Lydgate restores him in some measure to himself. And the carnally minded do not see everything there is either—however right Celia is about Casaubon, she misses a great deal that matters. But most important to bear in mind is that Dorothea *wants* to include the parish of Tipton in her ideal. It is simply not true she seeks intensity and greatness separate from the actual. She wants to realize them "here—now—in England."

Dorothea does not abjure the concrete. But such concrete goals as society offers a woman in her position cramp her. She would need to combine "girlish instruction comparable to the nibblings and judgments of a discursive mouse" (which she has) with "an endowment of stupidity and conceit" (which she has not), if she were to be satisfied with them. Then

> she might have thought that a Christian young lady of fortune
> should find her ideal of life in village charities, patronage of the
> humbler clergy, the perusal of "Female Scripture Characters"
> . . . and the care of her soul over her embroidery in her own
> boudoir—with a background of prospective marriage to a man
> who, if less strict than herself, as being involved in affairs reli-
> giously inexplicable, might be prayed for and seasonably ex-
> horted. From such contentment poor Dorothea was shut out.

The cramping narrowness of a woman's prospects is frequently conveyed in imagery of enclosure and compression: in Dorothea's dissatisfaction with the "walled-in maze of small paths that led no whither"—"so heavily did the world weight on her in spite of her independent energy"; in the description of her hopes for her first marriage—"she was going to have room for the energies which stirred uneasily under the dimness and pressure of her own ignorance and the petty peremptoriness of the world's habits."

But when she rejects narrow conventions in order to find room for her energies, her problem becomes the reverse of cramp—too much space. Her goals necessarily suffer from haziness of outline since they are not demarcated with the rigid precision of those offered ready-to-hand by society. Far from complacent in her vague ideals, Dorothea is aware from the first of this vagueness as a problem. "For a long while she had been oppressed by the indefiniteness which hung in her mind, like a thick summer haze, over all her desire to make her life greatly effective. What could she do, what ought she to do?" Worth considering in this connection is Dorothea's confusion at the wide vista of Rome. Her inability to seize upon any single object leaves her strength scattered and diffuse. Eliot shows that this confusion is as capable of obstructive effect as simple narrowness of outlook, for instance in the intriguing image of "a glut of confused ideas which check the flow of emotion." This is one of the "doubtful pains of discovering and marking out" one's own path.

Energy that produces no impact is energy squelched or diffused or redirected. Dorothea speaks at her uncle's table "with more energy than is expected of so young a lady." Mr. Brooke's response—"Young ladies don't understand political economy, you know"—comes like "an extinguisher over all her lights." But Dorothea has too much spark to be extinguished, and she wants anything but the haze of undirected energy, so she grasps at the closest objects of enthusiasm, Mr. Casaubon and his work. During the rest of the dinner she wants only to be left alone to hear him explain it. The rebound to Casaubon is shown again when Dorothea's cottage designing is dismissed by Celia as a fad. "The *fad* of drawing plans! What was life worth—what great faith was possible when the whole effect of one's actions could be withered up into such parched rubbish as that?" Not even Dorothea is a powerful enough personality to be exempt from the principle, shown repeatedly in *Middlemarch* and in all of George Eliot's works, that part of the way we see ourselves is the way we think others see us. This is why, for instance, Fred begins to feel more uncomfortably culpable when he imagines his culpability revealed to the Garths. Dorothea would need an obliviousness to others' opinions that even Savonarola lacks in *Romola*; the novel describes the self-doubt he feels when Florence turns against his work as inevitable to anyone without "a stupid inflexibility of self-confidence." "It always remains true that if we had been greater, circumstance would have been less strong against us." But how great can we be, facing "the hampering threadlike pressure of small social conditions, and their frustrating complexity"? Opinion is part of social conditions.

Tipton and Freshitt are "unfriendly mediums" to Dorothea. And "there is no creature whose inward being is so strong that it is not greatly determined by what lies outside it." When Dorothea rejoices in getting away from Tipton and Freshitt, she does not expect to transcend mediums, as some critics of her theoretic nature suggest. Rather she hopes for something friendlier in Lowick. The stymieing of energy in the scene with Celia prepares her for accepting Casaubon's proposal, as delivered in the next scene. Casaubon takes on the aspect of a winged messenger holding out his hand. He will give Dorothea the room she needs while at the same time saving her from the haze of her own indefiniteness. He offers "large yet definite duties."

He also offers entry into "those provinces of masculine knowledge"— Latin and Greek. Dorothea is interested in education because she believes it will remove the doubt of her own conclusions that adds to their haziness. While she casts herself in prospect in a self-subdued role as a wife, as her husband's lamp bearer and so on, she is hardly so selfless as she thinks. "She had not reached that point of renunciation at which she would have been satisfied with having a wise husband: she wished, poor child, to be wise herself." Caleb Garth says that no work can be done well if you mind what every fool says. "You must have it inside you that your plan is right." Dorothea has plans but not confidence that they are right. "She constantly doubted her own conclusions, because she felt her own ignorance: how could she be confident that one-roomed cottages were not for the glory of God, when men who knew the classics appeared to conciliate indifference to the cottages with zeal for the glory? Perhaps even Hebrew might be necessary." Hence her vulnerability to fools. She conceives of education as something that will enable her to act. She says to Sir James, "I am often unable to decide. But that is from ignorance. The right conclusion is there all the same, though I am unable to see it." Casaubon is to supply an object of action already decided and the means also of decisiveness on her own account. With him she can do something. Middlemarch has made, Middlemarch is, the conditions that make a poor dry mummified pedant appear to an ardent young woman who has seen nothing better as a sort of angel of vocation and of the education that enables vocation. Middlemarch need not smile on their union to bring it about.

The questions of vocation is central to *Middlemarch*. It is a question whose satisfactory answer lies not only, not even primarily, in what is done, but in the doing. The novel is one of the most psychologically profound literary investigations of the Victorian work ethic, for it shows that not to shape the world is to be shapeless oneself, which for natures conscious of shaping energy means painful consciousness of their own dis-

persal. Eliot says that her story does not simply tell the often-told romance
of man and woman, but the romance of vocation, of those who mean "to
shape their own deeds and alter the world a little." It hardly needs long
repeating that virtually all of the characters are engaged in the latter less-
celebrated but hardly less passionate romance: Dorothea, Lydgate, Casaubon, Bulstrode, Garth, Farebrother—though some of his passion has gone
over into resignation—and Fred Vincy—though he has the requisite passion supplied him by the expectations of his future wife, which is also to
some extent the case with Will Ladislaw. Even Rosamond Vincy can be
included in the list, though that will take some explaining later.

The intensity of the desire to do, to make, to count, that fills George
Eliot's people may be represented by two passages on what it is to fail of
fruition. When Casaubon is forced to give up his "Key to all Mythologies," he is presented as tragic, however little sublime his soul—"to re-
nounce a work which has been all the significance of its life—a significance
which is to vanish as the waters which come and go where no man has
need of them." When Lydgate must leave Middlemarch, he knows he
leaves "the new hospital [to] be joined with the old infirmary, and everything [to] go on as it might have done if I had never come." In both cases
the work that leaves no trace makes the self as if it had never been.

Lydgate's energy falls short of its task, as of course does the dim Casaubon's. But each man goes further with what he has than Dorothea can.
Casaubon finds motivation in the "outward requirements" of authorship
and marriage. Eliot often speaks of his "acquitting himself" in life. Lydgate's path comes less ready-made, but he has the direction and inspiration
of his education as well as the small increments of felt achievement that
reinforce his sense of strength and so carry him forward to further effort,
as in the beautiful and often-remarked image of the swimmer floating, for
whom even repose is no loss of impetus. Dorothea has only the meagerest
work in which to acquit herself and the meagerest education to help her
tread out her own path. Instead of being reinforced, her energy, which is
greater than anyone else's in the book, often fails to effect precisely because energy is not expected of a woman.

Eliot's analysis of this last failure is penetrating and subtle. She shows
that energy begins to relax when no impact results from effort. This accounts for Lydgate's slackening of will in the face of the impervious Rosamond. "Lydgate sat paralysed by opposing impulses: since no reasoning
he could apply to Rosamond seemed likely to conquer her assent, he
wanted to smash and grind some object on which he could at least produce
an impression, or else tell her brutally that he was master . . . . [but] the

very resolution to which he had wrought himself by dint of logic and honourable pride was beginning to relax under her torpedo contact." Any "mutual understanding and resolve . . . seemed blocked out by the sense of unsuccessful effort." Women are more subject to such paralysis than men because their efforts are more likely to be received as null, not wanted in the first place, and of no consequence when made.

A passage on Dorothea's life at Lowick after her return from Rome merits close analysis. The poor do not need her. Casaubon has not proved a teacher who will help her to be sure of her own schemes, but has rather discouraged them. She is shut out of his work first by himself and then by Will's revelation that the project is worthless. The result is a blank that begins to invade her sense of herself. Crucial here is the energy supply, which is threatened in two related ways. What is not called for may cease to be forthcoming, what sees no sign of its own power may grow powerless. The passage returns to the idea of indefiniteness. It figures this mental state again as one surrounded by a haze, here a "dun vapour," and combines what seems to be the opposed pair of liberty and oppression, understandable when liberty is merely lack of anything definite to do, which makes of the very width of the space a hampering medium. The more one can do anything one pleases, the more difficult is pleasing to do any one thing, or pleasing to do anything at all.

> Meanwhile there was the snow and the low arch of dun vapour—there was the stifling oppression of that gentlewoman's world, where everything was done for her and none asked for her aid—where the sense of connection with a manifold pregnant existence had to be kept up painfully as an inward vision, instead of coming from without in claims that would have shaped her energies.—"What shall I do?" "Whatever you please, my dear": that had been her brief history since she had left off learning morning lessons and practising silly rhythms on the hated piano. Marriage, which was to bring guidance into worthy and imperative occupation, had not yet freed her from the gentlewoman's oppressive liberty; it had not even filled her leisure with the ruminant joy of unchecked tenderness. Her blooming full-pulsed youth stood there in a moral imprisonment which made itself one with the chill, colourless, narrowed landscape, with the shrunken furniture, the never-read books, and the ghostly stag in a pale fantastic world that seemed to be vanishing from the daylight.

The passage also concerns the feeling of impotence that is a correlative of oppressive liberty. Consider the odd image of the vanishing stag. It is linked to the description in the paragraph that follows of Dorothea's nightmarish struggle "in which every object was withering and shrinking away from her." Later, Dorothea sees Will in the same terms, "receding into the distant world of warm activity and fellowship." He literally recedes from her when she passes him in her carriage; she feels that they are moving further and further apart and yet that she cannot stop. Such images of recession and loss of contact, of the self left stranded, are to be found in a curiously similar passage in "The Legend of Jubal," written while Eliot was working on *Middlemarch,* in 1870. It expresses "that dream-pain / Wherein the sense slips off from each loved thing / And all appearance is mere vanishing." What gives these lines special bearing for our understanding of Dorothea is that they are part of a description of the bewilderment of Jubal's sense of his identity. When the singing crowd fails to recognize him as the creator of song, his power of impact is thrown into question. Things seem slipping away from him and so too does his very self.

Dorothea approaches a disorientation and despair that resembles Armgart's in the poem of that name, also written by Eliot in 1870, which in its treatment of a woman's failed vocation is a study in themes worked out at length in *Middlemarch.* With the loss of her superb voice and her power to move audiences Armgart feels "I can do nought / Better than what a million women do— / Must drudge among the crowd and feel my life / Beating upon the world without response." Her feeling of impotence is beautifully captured in the image of a classical statue whose every line expresses energy but energy that cannot touch its mark because the instrumental arms are missing: "A Will / That, like an arm astretch and broken off, / Has nought to hurl—the torso of a soul." Armgart wants to die rather than get used to her ordinary woman's lot because if she did, her life would not be beating even in frustration. She feels she would have lost herself.

The "manifold pregnant existence" from which Dorothea feels disconnected includes a sense of her own existence, for the passage insists on the shaping force of outward things for the energies that reach out to shape the world. Outward claims elicit energy as well as shape it. Outward manifestation confirms energy and keeps it coming. Dorothea's life is a prospect "full of motiveless ease—motiveless, if her own energy could not seek out reasons for ardent action." The worst danger of ease is that it leave one motiveless. Worse than reaching out to touch things that shrink and wither away would be no longer reaching out to touch at all.

Everyone comments on George Eliot's celebration of duty and work and the renunciation of self in favor of some worthy object. Most concentrate on the content of that duty or work: what is the worthy object? Answers can be found, but they skip over an important point, which is Eliot's deep concern with the human need for duty, work, or object, whose worthiness is to be measured as much by the sense of worth it can confer upon the man or woman who strives for it as by its independent content.

For all her criticism of the shabby devices of egoism, Eliot never suggests that there is any way of transcending it. *Middlemarch*'s famous pier glass, with its random scratches revealed as particular patterns by the light of particular beholders, is a parable even for those who, like Dorothea, are capable of imagining how differently the light must fall for someone else. Even in the latter image, used to describe Dorothea's realization that Casaubon has his own separate center of self, there is no suggestion that she can see exactly as he sees or know that difference first hand. It suggests the limitations of her own ego at the same time that those limits expand in the act of imagining another's. I think what is emancipating about the idea is not that she can transcend herself, but that in partly, only partly, imagining another self she can imagine herself as making a difference in the way the light falls for him. She can imagine herself as making part of the pattern that his candle illuminates. To make a difference in this way is less crude than other ways of fulfilling egoism, but it is a way. In *Architects of the Self* Calvin Bedient pounces on the egoistic implications of empathy and altruism as if he had made a great discovery of the philosophical George Eliot's inconsistency, the moral George Eliot's self-delusion. But evidence in addition to *Middlemarch* itself can be offered that she knows what she is saying and means to say it—that one works out of one's own pressing need as well as the world's.

An extremely interesting letter of December 10, 1874 to Mrs. Ponsonby answers the question of how to combat the feeling of futility that accompanies loss of belief in god and immortality. The danger is "petrified volition," Eliot says. She advises cultivating the imagination of others' needs and altruistic work, which will liberate this volition: "we can say to ourselves with effect, 'There is an order of considerations which I will keep myself continually in mind of, so that they may continually be the prompters of certain feelings and actions.' " A letter of October 2, 1876 to Madame Eugène Bodichon also casts the weight of its argument upon the value of altruism for the purpose it gives rather than the purpose it serves. This time Eliot addresses herself to women's purpose: "Yes. Women can do much for the other women (and men) to come. My impression of the good there is in all unselfish efforts is continually strengthened. Doubtless many a ship is drowned on expeditions of discovery of rescue, and precious freights lie buried. But there was the good of manning and furnishing the ship with a great purpose before it set out."

In a letter of November 4, 1872 to Alexander Main upon the completion of *Middlemarch* Eliot describes her satisfaction. She considers the work's value separately from its intrinsic worth. She is at peace with it not because it is perfect but because in it she was able to do as perfectly as she could. Yet the impulse to work flags without some faith in the value of the result. This is why in another letter to Main of May 26, 1875 she speaks of the paralyzing impression bad art makes on her. "Great art, in any kind, inspirits me and makes me feel the worth of devoted effort, but from bad pictures, bad books, vulgar music, I come away with a paralyzing depression." Ruby Redinger's recent biography shows how subject Eliot was to such paralysis of initiative. She needed constant validation of the independent worth of her work—from Lewes, from friends and reviewers, from her books' popularity, even as measured by sales and receipts—to such an extent that Lewes learned to filter through to her only those responses that could give her the validation that kept her working.

Dorothea experiences a dismay similar to Eliot's own at the sight of bad art in Rome. Bad art is the vanity of effort made visible. The pictures suggest objectified lives, which would look equally ugly and bungling if hung on the wall. Dorothea suffers the collapse of impulse that this comparison of art and life implies. For once, instead of giving out ardor with little return, she needs to be fed with somebody else's ardor. But Will's encouragement misses the mark on an essential point. Their discussion of art turns to poets, and he says that to be a poet is to possess a certain state of feeling and intellect. This fails to satisfy Dorothea. She says the poems "are wanted to complete the poet." Possessing a poetic state of mind is no consolation because "I am sure I could never produce a poem." This is Carlyle's "produce, produce!" or Mary Garth's "might, could, would—they are contemptible auxiliaries." It is the Victorian work ethic understood without the crassness of the merely materialistic or utilitarian, for it locates in the product the motive to self-completion.

Will says that if Dorothea is no poet because she cannot produce a poem, she is herself a poem. She is pleased by this, which at first surprised me since it is no fulfillment of that "idea of some active good within her reach [that] 'haunted her like a passion.' " It seems so passive. But Dorothea must be consoled where she can, and I think the consolation here is the thought of the difference she makes in the consciousness that might make the poems, in a word, the difference she makes to Will. She enjoys the idea that she has a little kingdom in him, that he is willing to be swayed by her, when she has generally found very little room in other people's minds for what she has to say. He is the one person she has found to be receptive. Will does not please only because his eyes give out light, but because his eyes tell her that not the smallest movement of her own passes unnoticed, which realization "came like a pleasant glow to Dorothea."

John Halperin interprets this glow as the sign of Dorothea's discovery that "she is a woman who needs a man," which is true in a way that he pays very little attention to, that is, what she needs him *for*. For one thing, and it is not a little thing, she needs him for the testament he gives her of her own power. The glow signals a movement towards hope in that near-despairing meditation on the stifling oppression of a gentlewoman's life, called "vivid." It does not turn her away from her husband as one would imagine ordinary love for another man would do, and Halperin seems to have something very ordinary in mind. Rather, it turns her towards him, with a hope that formulates itself in a reversal of the nightmare images of a world receding from her touch—that is, in hope of impact: "She felt as if all her morning's gloom would vanish if she could see her husband glad because of her presence." Here we see the lapse between vague ideals and "the common yearning of womanhood," and we see the reason for it. Failing everything else, Dorothea falls back on "the ardent woman's need to rule beneficently by making the joy of another soul." That this is work, with the same psychological benefits at stake as in any other form, is illustrated by the fact that Dorothea experiences the same sensations at the unresponsiveness of Casaubon's arm when she takes it as he does at Carp's dismissal of his publications.

Women's work is men: a tired old saying, but full of fine insight in Eliot's treatment, or perhaps three fine insights. She shows that men are just about all the work women have and little enough for some large souls; she shows that making the *joy* of another soul is by no means its only form; and she shows the void that threatens should this work too be cut off. All three follow in ways Middlemarch would never expect from its easy assumption that as the world can pretty much do without the work of women, women can pretty much do without work.

Dorothea illustrates the first point. On the next two points let us turn to Mary Garth and Rosamond Vincy. Mary makes considerably more than Fred's joy. To all intents and purposes she makes Fred. She is the audience whose demand for the best supplies his deficiency of self-activating enterprise. Mr. Garth says a good woman's love "shapes many a rough fellow," and Mr. Farebrother reflects that "to win her may be a discipline." Dorothea's high expectations of others also provide the motive and channel to effort that women often supply but very seldom enjoy. In her believing conception Lydgate salvages something of his best self, and without her love Will would give up trying to amount to anything more than a dilettante.

Rosamond does not the less make Lydgate what he finally is for concerning herself not at all with the joy of his soul. It is abundantly clear that she has energy and a will. She is as "industrious" in her way as other characters; her ideas too have "shaping activity." One can almost discern in Rosamond the makings of a feminist of the most literal-minded sort, for she is introduced in the novel as someone who sees no reason why Fred should get his way any more than she should: "I cannot see why brothers are to make themselves disagreeable, any more than sisters." She displays no feminist rejection of a woman's scope of action though, throwing all her will and energy into achieving the daintiest wardrobe and the highest-ranking, best-providing husband. In view of the doubtful pains it costs a woman to mark out anything more original, and in view of the odds against learning a taste for originality, or pains, at Miss Lemon's school, we are not invited to blame Rosamond with as much cold dislike as most critics permit themselves.

I think a case can be made for some sympathy with Rosamond, even while we respond to the pathos of Lydgate's losing struggle with Middlemarch, of whose meshes she represents a particularly strangling coil. If she removes the house from the market without consulting him, he put it on without consulting her. The justice on his side is smaller, even according to Middlemarch standards of wifely versus husbandly prerogative, when he becomes angry at her for sending out invitations without consultation. This is surely a wife's right. If the invitations are ill-timed, it is because he failed to tell her of the disgrace that makes them so. But Eliot's bid for our sympathy with Rosamond depends less on our feeling that she is wronged than on our understanding that the wrong she does proceeds from her position as a woman.

Her petty manuevers seem less blameworthy when we consider how little else she has to do. Again and again Eliot reminds us of how much time Rosamond has to fill. The "elegant leisure of a young lady's mind," if not occupied with something, leaves her "wondering what she should do next." Lydgate is bitter when he asks himself, "what can a woman care about so much as house and furniture?" but it is a question that goes to the heart of the matter. Eliot shows that a main cause of the failure of their marriage is one of Lydgate's "spots of commonness." This spot is indeed common; if it were less so Rosamond would not be what she is. Lydgate completely fails to imagine that he himself becomes her work by default. "It had not occurred to Lydgate that he had been a subject of eager meditation to Rosamond, who had neither any reason for throwing her marriage into distant perspective, nor any pathological studies to divert her mind from that ruminating habit, that inward repetition of looks, words, and phrases, which makes a large part in the lives of most girls." In the same scene in which Lydgate expresses his deep need to do and to be recognized for what he does—"What good is like to this, / To do worthy the writing, and to write / Worthy the reading and the world's delight?"—he wonders why Rosamond has no "ambition." But what he means by ambition in a woman is that she should want her husband to achieve much.

Lydgate's theory of women as beings providentially framed to live in and through their husbands in this way is met by the refuting irony that Rosamond does not identify with him at all, as becomes clear during his troubles. He expects that women should find fulfillment through a vicariousness that his own experience, indeed all of *Middlemarch,* puts to question. For when women fulfill their need for vocation through men, they do so through their effect on the men, not through the men's independent achievements. Rosamond knows that the area of Lydgate's work is not one in which she makes a great deal of difference. When he is ruminating on his work, "Rosamond's presence at that moment was perhaps no more than a spoonful brought to the lake, and her woman's instinct in this matter was not dull." Rosamond can be more measurably effective towards house and furniture than towards discovery of the primitive tissue, and if we are not charmed to see her aiming at these things, we can hardly feel the surprise necessary for outrage. When women have no work but men and men do not even realize it, two things may follow. One is that a man may find the romance of vocation disrupted by the romance of the sexes—as Lydgate does. The other is that a woman may find marriage itself the condition of discontent, more than the particular husband—as Rosamond does.

We see the result in Rosamond's ordinary nature of the same narrow scope offered women which has very different consequences in an extraordinary nature like Dorothea's. Both feel energy and will in want of something to do, both find their work in men, both know the void of meaning, the devastation of self, that threaten should these men prove impervious. This last point is most explicitly presented in Rosamond's case. When Will turns on her and destroys her presumption of romantic rule, she "was almost losing the sense of her identity."

Rosamond collapses into a torpor of the same kind that Dorothea faces in the nonresponse of Casaubon. Why do anything that will only read back to you your own incompetence?—"What [Dorothea] dreaded was to exert herself in reading or anything else which left him as joyless as ever." Eliot returns repeatedly to the idea of arrest of energy by premonition of impotence, showing Dorothea's "nightmare of a life [with Casaubon] in which every energy was arrested by dread," "a perpetual struggle of energy with fear." "Her ardour, continually repulsed, served, with her intense memory, to heighten her dread, as thwarted energy subsides into a shudder." The last is a striking image of energy defeated of outward impact, turning back upon itself. Dorothea's nature has too much force to lose it all in torpor. She learns "timidity," but hardly the passive kind. Her "self-repression," her "resolved submission" are strenuous. A good instance of the effort of motionlessness is her constraining herself to lie still in bed lest she should wake her husband. Eliot shows the energy that goes into "shut[ting] her best soul in prison . . . that she might be petty enough to please him." She also shows the reason—that for a woman in Dorothea's position, constraint of her best soul, which might otherwise have acted to the highest account, is the only way to count at all.

Dorothea does count. She produces a movement of human fellowship in Casaubon. She does the same with Rosamond after a struggle to subdue the claims of self, which if somewhat different in its occasion, is very similar in its psychological movement. She wrings motive out of despair: "She said to her own irremediable grief, that it should make her more helpful, instead of driving her back from effort." Dorothea knows that her power of making an effort is a precious resource, and one that can be lost. She understands her troubles as specifically a woman's. She says to Will,

> I had no notion . . . of the unexpected way in which trouble comes, and ties our hands, and makes us silent when we long to speak. I used to despise women a little for not shaping their lives more, and doing better things. I was very fond of doing as I liked, but I have almost given it up.

An indication of how much Dorothea has given up is that she has given up even certain ways of talking—is silent where she used to speak. According to Derek Oldfield's fascinating linguistic analysis, her unchecked idiom is characterized by exclamations, declarative assertions, imperatives, simple, direct sentences often beginning with "I." He is especially acute in showing the atrophy of her figurative mode of speaking and her curious shift from questions posed so as to elicit a "yes" response to rhetorical questions that really demand no response at all.

Another instance of Dorothea's growing inhibition is in the way she moves—as if her hands were tied. This can be seen in her interviews with Will, which become progressively more stilted. They are conducted at a significant distance. Eliot specifies the distance—two yards, one yard. "She looked at him from that distance"; "Dorothea looked at him from that distance." He sits on one settee, she on another. When she moves to the window, he does not follow, or he moves away from it. These scenes are painful because they have so much emotion and so little motion: "She looked as if there were a spell upon her, keeping her motionless and hindering her from unclasping her hands, while some intense, grave yearning was imprisoned within her eyes"; "they were like two creatures slowly turning to marble in each other's presence, while their hearts were conscious and their eyes were yearning."

On the level of action Dorothea comes closest to giving up altogether when she decides to acquiesce in Casaubon's request that she carry on his work after his death. This would truly be work to no avail in that, as we have seen, the only avail to which Dorothea works is Casaubon himself, the living man. Significantly, the decision for this self-sacrifice is attended by a "passivity which was unusual with her." Dorothea comes uncharacteristically close to torpor. It seems that only circumstances can save her from this fate, "so heavily did the world weigh on her in spite of her independent energy." Casaubon dies. Dorothea is liberated from the "strain and conflict of self-repression"—but only to emerge into "another sort of pinfold than that form which she had been released."

Does Dorothea escape from this pinfold when she takes the initiative and marries Will despite Middlemarch? I think not entirely, for the tone of regret is strong in the finale, even if it is a regret for what could hardly be helped. Dorothea's fate represents a sacrifice, only less sad than it might have been. When Eliot says that "many . . . thought it a pity that so substantive and rare a creature should have been absorbed into the life of another . . . . But no one stated exactly what else that was in her power she ought rather to have done," she points to the limits of power for an individual not helped by her medium.

Dorothea is not a nineteenth-century Saint Theresa. The blocking of the channels to deeds is also the diffusion or retreat of the character who might have done them, hence the "inconvenient indefiniteness" of even the most impressive women, or their lapse into "the common yearning of womanhood." Dorothea achieves the definite at the expense of her highest potential, which is too vague to be of much good to her or the world. In explaining her decision to marry Will she says, "I might have done something better, if I had been better. But this is what I am going to do." I think *Middlemarch* shows that Dorothea would have *been* better if she had been in a position to *do* better. George Eliot does not allow us the sentimental consolation of contemplating great souls trapped in an insignificant universe; souls that do not contribute significantly lose some of their greatness. Lydgate feels this in his own case. While less her own fault, the loss is felt in Dorothea's case too. In her essay on Margaret Fuller and Mary Wollstonecraft, Eliot commends the two feminists for not idealizing women. What argues a need for women's emancipation is their present debasement, she says, not their excellence in all virtues.

While generally recognizing that Dorothea hardly liberates herself from Middlemarch to the extent of epic action, opinion varies as to the scope of her pinfold and the amount of satisfaction we are to feel in it. At the center of this debate is Will Ladislaw. Many early reviewers were disappointed in Dorothea's marriage to Will, as were early readers such as those Eliot describes in a letter to John Blackwood of September 19, 1873: Two ladies came up to her at Oxford; one wondered how she could let Dorothea marry that Casaubon, while the other said Ladislaw was just as bad. Will is often criticized as inadequate for his impressive wife. Henry James, Leslie Stephen, Lord David Cecil, and Walter Allen speak for the view that Eliot is carried away by her own fondness for him. Jerome Thale at least gives her credit for a lapse in artistic control rather than a lapse in her taste in men. He thinks Will's weakness is not to be held to the account of authorial indulgence but of insufficient development. The feminist critic Patricia Beer reverses the usual analysis by saying that it is a distaste for Will as a conceited dilettante that Eliot "cannot help" expressing, though intending otherwise. All of this criticism is based on the assumption that the author means Will to be a match for Dorothea but goes wrong. Calvin Bedient states the assumption baldly, that *Middlemarch* is "a book that has written itself," that the theme has Eliot "helplessly and almost mindlessly in its spell." In the face of the overwhelming intelligence of the author and the systematic, even laborious cast of her mind, which hardly anybody fails to mention—to the unsympathetic, like William Ernest Henley, her books read like "the fruit of a caprice of Apollo for the Differential Calculus"—and in the face of the deliberateness of the construction of *Middlemarch,* shown in studies by Anna Theresa Kitchel and Jerome Beaty, I think this assumption deserves little credit.

Some critics have taken the other course of concluding that since Eliot ends her book with a second marriage better than the first, she must mean it to be the final solution. Foremost among these are the believers in marriage and the family and the woman finding her man, those whom one might expect to be Victorians but who are not necessarily. But Eliot's ironies at the expense of the third-volume marriage in "Silly Novels by Lady Novelists" indicate that she did *not* always think of marriage as "that desirable consummation."

I place myself among the small number of critics for whom R. H. Hutton speaks in 1873: "one feels, and is probably meant to feel acutely, that here too, it is 'the meanness of opportunity' and not intrinsic suitability, which determines Dorothea's second comparatively happy marriage." Will is a slight creature beside her. Surely we are meant to feel this, for instance, when Eliot follows the climactic chapter on Dorothea's noble resolve in going to Rosamond by one that opens with Will, whose resolve is "a state of mind liable to melt into a minuet with other states of mind, and to find itself bowing, smiling, and giving place with polite facility." Will combines his own limitations with certain assumptions about the limitations of women, so that his resemblance to Mr. Brooke, Sir James, Lydgate, and Casaubon sometimes becomes uncomfortable. He can be as put off by her power and eloquence as any of them. Eliot says of him, "A man is seldom ashamed of feeling that he cannot love a woman so well when he sees a certain greatness in her: nature having intended greatness for men." Two things he does love in her are her innocent shortsightedness and her inaccessibility. He would almost rather do without her love than that she should be sullied by recognizing the obvious fact of his feelings for her and the implications of Casaubon's jealousy. Also, "what others might have called the futility of his passion, made an additional delight for his imagination." His pedestal theory—Dorothea is "enthroned in his soul" as per the "higher love-poetry"—is sometimes experienced by Dorothea as a problem. She in her carriage, passing him on foot, "felt a pang at being seated there in a sort of exaltation, leaving him behind." One wonders if she does not lose a bit of her charm for him in delivering herself from the pedestal into his arms, just as she does in speaking with unfeminine greatness. Will is not exempt from some of the attitudes that contribute to the meanness of a woman's opportunity. At the same time the very irresoluteness and flexibility that make him slight make him impressionable. He can take the pressure of other people's thought. And Dorothea certainly needs to make a mark somewhere.

Any discussion of the scope and satisfaction we are to attribute to

Dorothea's final lot should turn on her husband's work as well as his character, for we know that she gives him wifely help in it. This issue is too seldom addressed, whether by those who think a husband is enough or by those who think he is not. Michael York Mason is right in saying that critics have not dwelt enough on *Middlemarch* as a historical novel that evokes the past in relation to the present. The present for Eliot's readers was the recent passage of the second Reform Bill. *Middlemarch* treats the period of the first, and though it ends with its defeat, the historical perspective that shows this to be but temporary is built into the novel; for instance, to locate the story in "ante-reform times" is to locate it in relation to the ultimate passage of reform. Dorothea, through a husband who works for this passage, contributes something to a movement that is not defeated and that qualifies, as much as Saint Theresa's reform of a religious order, as a "far-resonant action." The importance of Reform is I think a given. To understand it is part of the necessary equipment for reading the novel. Eliot ranks it as one of the momentous events of the period in her notebook. We can trust to Felix Holt as a spokesman for her political views, more so than is usually safe when it comes to fictional characters, since Eliot used his persona in a separate nonfictional political article for the *Westminster Review* in 1868. Felix Holt is for Reform. He says he would despise any man not interested in the great political movement of the time. His friend and fellow radical calls it a "massive achievement." Will Ladislaw emerges with the upper hand in contending against Lydgate that the Bill must be passed, even if it is done without immaculate political tools. Whatever Eliot's reservations about the transaction of Reform, there is no doubt that she holds it part of "the growing good of the world." While the reader's hopefulness in response to the end of *Middlemarch* should be somewhat dashed in Will Ladislaw, it should take some heart in Reform.

It is interesting that the feminist critics are even more depressed by the novel's end than most, and more than they need be. Neither Abba Goold Woolson in the 1880s nor Lee Edwards or Patricia Beer in the 1970s pays any attention to Reform. Woolson and Edwards are disappointed that Eliot makes a woman who might have been great come to so little; Beer thinks it is unnecessarily little. Woolson reproaches Eliot for suggesting that a heroine must fail when some real women did not; Edwards and Beer point out that Eliot herself did not.

Exasperation with heroines who are not models of success turns up frequently in feminist criticism. When Harriet Rosenstein excoriates Elizabeth Hardwick's book *Seduction and Betrayal* for seeming to endorse a literary tradition that dignifies women by measure of their tragic calamity, she implies a contrary ideal of what the woman novelist should write. Woolson supplies a description of the ideal, to which, in less Victorian terms, many modern feminists seem to subscribe: "From the fictitious scenes upon her pages, her gifted sisters will gather inspiration and hope, to quicken all their brave endeavors after good. For she will picture their advancing life, not as a gloomy valley, into which their pathways must descend through ever-deepening shades, till existence closes in endless night, but as a broadening upland, along whose sweet ascents they are summoned to pass, with bounding steps and uplifted gaze."

George Eliot does not show her heroine summoned to sweet ascent, but surely to supply such a satisfactory summons would be to endanger realism. I agree with Ruth Yeazell when she chides critics for expecting literary pictures of strong women succeeding in a period that did not make them likely in life. As Virginia Woolf says, George Eliot stuck to the sad facts. And yet everything that is not a broadening upland is not necessarily endless night. Lee Edwards is too quick to decide that *Middlemarch* "can no longer be one of the books of my life."

If I examine my own feeling upon finishing *Middlemarch,* I do not find depression predominant, I think a simple but important reason for this is that if the main characters all slip below their own intention (except Mr. Garth with his fences), the novel does not. I am venturing a reason here that I know may seem to stretch thin because it can be made to cover so much. What great work cannot be said to redeem sad content by the inspiration of its artistry? But then again, is there not a particular triumph of form in a work so acutely concerned with the forces of dispersal? I think the idea bears considering, at least briefly.

Most critics recognize in George Eliot's works a strong narrative control and, further, a control that not only operates but makes itself felt. In fact a standard complaint is against her insistence as a narrator. She generalizes, she judges, she philosophizes, she aphorizes, she moralizes. Those who resist this intrusive narrative persona, whom they would rather see disappear behind the characters, attest to its power. I have noticed that power is a word much used in criticism of George Eliot. It is a commonplace of critical discourse, certainly, but I think it is often applied rather literally to Eliot. Sidney Colvin's essay offers a good example. He keeps coming back to the "overwhelming power," the "potency" and "trenchancy" of the style. He phrases the idea to suggest also that the style is "displaying its power," that the potency and trenchancy are "equally subtle and equally sure of themselves." Quentin Anderson says, "when one is reading *Middlemarch* there are many moments when one looks up and says, 'How intelligent, how penetrating this woman is!'" I know exactly what he means, and I believe most readers know.

Eliot's potency draws attention to itself. I, at least, am struck by the fact that there is nothing glutinous about the expanse of *Middlemarch*, by marked contrast to Mr. Brooke's desultoriness. The unfolding of its eighty-six chapters, prelude, and finale, follows a principle of human speech different from the usual, which is to say what one has said before. How can Eliot keep up for so long the precision, density, and force of her images and phrases?—memory as "the ordinary long-used blotting-book which only tells of forgotten writing"; Mr. Casaubon's benighted labors— "in bitter manuscript remarks on other men's notions about the solar deities, he had become indifferent to the sunlight"; Rosamond's pettiness, in whose mind "there was not room enough for luxuries to look small in." The spectacle of Rome is "a disease of the retina"; to be sensitive to ordinary human suffering would be to "die of that roar which lies on the other side of silence." There is something noticeably strenuous here. George Eliot is as strenuous as her characters. Anderson thinks that she is present as the most fully realized individual in *Middlemarch*. Isobel Armstrong thinks she is chorus to her own novel.

From this point of view the narrator may be seen to play counterpart to the characters. Where they fail, she succeeds, and I think we feel it, palpably, on every page. *Middlemarch* itself is a testament to the possibility of "far-resonant action," and "long-recognizable deed." No feminist need feel disappointed.

Recognizing Casaubon

Neil Hertz

About halfway through *Middlemarch,* after having described one more manifestation of Mr. Casaubon's preoccupying self-concern, the narrator goes on to add a more general reflection:

> Will not a tiny speck very close to our vision blot out the glory of the world, and leave only a margin by which we see the blot? I know no speck so troublesome as self.

The remark is characteristic of George Eliot in a number of ways, most obviously in its ethical implications: egotism in her writings is almost always rendered as narcissism, the self doubled and figured as both the eye and the blot. But equally typical is the care with which a particular image is introduced and its figurative possibilities developed. The speck blots out the glory of the world: that in itself would have enforced the moral. But the trope is given a second turn: the glory of the world illuminates the margin—the effect is of a sort of halo of light—but only so as to allow us all the better to see the blot. The intelligence at work extending a line of figurative language brings it back, with a nice appropriateness, to the ethical point. This is an instance of the sort of metaphorical control that teacher-critics have always admired in *Middlemarch,* the sign of a humane moral consciousness elaborating patterns of action and imagery with great inventiveness and absolutely no horsing around. Many a telling demonstration—in print and in the classroom, especially in the classroom—of the extraliterary value of formal analysis has been built around passages like this.

But what about that blot and its margin? Is the figurative language

---

From *Glyph* 6 (1979). © 1979 by The Johns Hopkins University Press.

here so firmly anchored in a stable understanding of the moral relations of the self that it can't drift off in the direction of other margins and other blots?

I have in mind two specific citations, both associated with Mr. Casaubon early in the novel. At one point George Eliot's heroine, Dorothea, is seen in her library "seated and already deep in one of the pamphlets which had some marginal manuscript of Mr. Casaubon's"; at another, Casaubon's pedantically accurate memory is compared to "a volume where a *vide supra* could serve instead of repetitions, and not the ordinary long-used blotting-book which only tells of forgotten writing." It might be objected that the blot we've been considering is clearly not an inkblot, the margin clearly not the margin of a printed page; that indeed it is only by ruling out those meanings as extraneous to this particular context that we can visualize the image at all—this image of vision, of obstructed vision, of some small physical object coming between one's eyes and the world. Of course: the image, to remain an image, must restrict the range of figurative meaning we allow to the words that compose it. And, given that restraining function, it seems all the more appropriate that the image here is operating to clarify an ethical point about the self, just as it is appropriate that the tag "the moral imagination" has been so popular a way of referring to George Eliot's particular powers as a writer.

And yet, between themselves, those words *blot* and *margin* work to encourage just such a misreading of the image they nevertheless define and are defined by: *blot* helps us hear a rustle of paper in *margin, margin* makes *blot* sound just a bit inkier. And both, as it happens, are easily drawn out of their immediate context by the cumulative force of a series of less equivocal allusions to handwriting, printing, writing in general, all clustered about the figure of Casaubon. One character refers to him as a "sort of parchment code," another wisecracks "Somebody put a drop [of his blood] under a magnifying glass, and it was all semi-colons and parentheses," his own single lugubrious attempt at a joke turns on "a word that has dropped out of the text," and there are more serious and consequential allusions of the same sort. Earlier in their acquaintance, when Dorothea is most taken with her husband-to-be, Eliot writes: "He was all she had at first imagined him to be: almost everything he had said seemed like a specimen from a mine, or the inscription on the door of a museum which might open on the treasure of past ages." Later, in Rome, after the first quarrel of their marriage, Dorothea accompanies him to the Vatican, walking with him "through the stony avenue of inscriptions" and leaving him at the entrance to the library. Back in England, in their own library, after another quarrel, Mr. Casaubon tries to resume work, but "his hand trembled so much that the words seemed to be written in an unknown character."

In the past, when critics have directed attention to such passages it has been either to comment on the general appropriateness of these images to Mr. Casaubon—who is, after all, a scholar—or on the particular finesse with which one image or another is adjusted to the unfolding drama of the Casaubons' marriage. More recently J. Hillis Miller, citing a pair of similar passages, both about Dorothea's wildly mistaken first impressions of her husband, has stressed the nondramatic value of these allusions: Casaubon, he notes, "is a text, a collection of signs which Dorothea misreads, according to that universal propensity for misinterpretation which infects all the characters in *Middlemarch*." Miller is right about Casaubon, but the point he would make is still more inclusive: he is arguing for a reading of the novel that would see every character as simultaneously an interpreter (the word is a recurrent one in *Middlemarch*) and a text available for the interpretations (plural, always partial, and often in conflict) of others. It is with reference to Lydgate, he could have pointed out, and not to Casaubon, that George Eliot writes that a man may "be known merely as a cluster of signs for his neighbors' false suppositions."

Miller's argument is persuasive, and the reading of the novel he sketches is a bold and attractive one: he takes *Middlemarch* to be simultaneously affirming the values of Victorian humanism which it has been traditionally held to affirm—for example, a belief in the consistence of the self as a moral agent—and systematically under-cutting those values, offering in place of an ethically stable notion of the self the somewhat less reassuring figure of a focus of semiotic energy, receiving and interpreting signs, itself a "cluster of signs" more or less legible. Miller's movement toward this poised, deconstructive formulation, however, is condensed and rapid, and may still leave one wondering how those two notions of the self are held in suspension in the novel, and what the commerce is between them. In the pages that follow I propose to take up that question by dwelling on the figure of Casaubon, and by asking what it might mean, if *all* the characters in *Middlemarch* may be thought of as texts or as clusters of signs, for the signs of textuality to cluster so thickly around one particular name. Or, to put it another way, why is Mr. Casaubon made to seem not merely an especially sterile and egotistical person, but at moments like a quasi-allegorical figure, the personification of the dead letter, the written word? Personifications exist somewhere in the middle ground between realistically represented persons and configurations of signs: that would seem to be ground worth going over. But I want to approach it obliquely, by first considering some passages where it is not Casaubon, but George Eliot herself—not the blot but the eye—around whom are clustered the signs of egotism and of writing.

I

Reading through Eliot's early letters one comes across—not on every page, but often enough to catch one's attention—a particular kind of apology. In one, for example, written when she was nineteen, she concludes with these lines:

> I have written at random and have not said all I wanted to say. I hope the frequent use of the personal pronoun will not lead you to think that I suppose it to confer any weight on what I have said. I used it to prevent circumlocution and waste of time. I am ashamed to send a letter like this as if I thought more highly of myself than I ought to think, which is alas! too true.

And then, beneath her signature, as a second thought, a postscript:

> In reading my letter I find difficulties in understanding my scribble that I fear are hopelessly insurmountable for another.

Typically, apologies for what she fears may seem like egotism are accompanied by apologies for her handwriting:

> I . . . hope that you will be magnanimous enough to forgive the trouble my almost indecipherable letter will give you. Do not, pray, write neatly to me, for I cannot undertake to correspond with any one who will not allow me to scribble, though this precious sheet has, I think, an extra portion of untidiness.

> I have written an almost unpardonably egotistical letter to say nothing of its other blemishes.

> Tell me if you have great trouble in making out my cabalistic letters: if you have, I will write more deliberately next time.

The feeling behind these apologies need not be either particularly strong or particularly sincere: often they are perfunctory, or positively comical, as in this passage, where jokes about handwriting oddly prefigure the language that will be associated with Casaubon thirty years later:

You will think me interminably loquacious, and still worse you will be ready to compare my scribbled sheet to the walls of an Egyptian tomb for mystery, and determine not to imitate certain wise antiquaries or antiquarian wiseacres who "waste their precious years, how soon to fail?" in deciphering information which has only the lichen and moss of age to make it more valuable than facts graphically conveyed by an upholsterer's pattern book.

What's curious is the stress not simply on the messiness of what she calls her "scribble," but on its cabalistic or hieroglyphic indecipherability. The point might be that language turns opaque and resistant when it is too purely in the service of self, when self-expressive scribbles replace legible communicating signs. In that case these apologies for sloppy handwriting might be read as slight nervous displacements of the apologies for egotism they accompany. But there is more going on here than that: writing, like the self-doubling of narcissism, is disturbing not simply because it may seem "self-centered" but because it is both that and self-dispersing at once.
When handwriting is legible it becomes not only available to others but transparent—and attractive—as self-expression, seemingly adequate in its relation to whatever it is the self would exteriorize. At such moments one's sense of the distance between one's self and the signs one produces can be cheerfully ignored or even enjoyed. And in fact an instance of just such enjoyment—narcissistic through and through, and thoroughly engaging—can be discerned in what is, by a happy accident, the earliest bit of Eliot's writing to have survived. It is to be found on the cover of a school notebook she used when she was fourteen, a notebook which contains some arithmetic exercises, an essay on "affectation and conceit," the beginnings of a story in the manner of Sir Walter Scott, some poems she'd copied out, some drawings, and so forth. But on its cover, in a large, flourishing, ornate script, is a date—"March 16th 1834"—and a name: "Marianne Evans." It is her signature, but not quite her name, for she was christened Mary Anne, not Marianne. Gordon Haight, who reprints parts of the notebook in an appendix to his biography, remarks that she was learning French at the time, as well as being trained, as was the custom in girls' schools, in elegant penmanship: the combination seems to have produced this striking emblem of a writer's beginnings, the schoolgirls' slight, slightly romantic alteration of her name, written out large and with care, there to be contemplated on the cover of her book, the space of musing reverie opening up between herself and her signature, a space in which a certain play of transformation becomes plausible.

Sometimes that space is welcomed as a "breathing-space," or, in a favorite image of George Eliot's, as "room" into which she can "expand"; at those moments the writing that structures that space stops being "scribble" and becomes what she likes to call "utterance," drawing on the Pentecostal associations of that word:

> It is necessary to me not simply to *be* but to *utter,* and I require utterance of my friends . . . . It is like a diffusion or expansion of one's own life to be assured that its vibrations are repeated in another, and words are the media of those vibrations. How can you say that music must end in silence? Is not the universe itself a perpetual utterance of the One Being?

But these moments of expansive utterance, where neither the distance between the self and its signs nor the difference between selves is felt as a problem, are commonly followed in George Eliot's texts by moments of anxious "shrinking" and remorse:

> I feel a sort of madness growing upon me—just the opposite of the delirium which makes people fancy that their bodies are filling the room. It seems to me as if I were shrinking into that mathematical abstraction, a point—so entirely am I destitute of contact that I am unconscious of length and breadth.

This alternation between exuberance and apology, expansion and shrinking, utterance and scribble, was to govern Eliot's literary production throughout her life: she lived it as a rhythm of fluctuating excitement and discouragement while she was working on her novels, followed by deep gloom when each was completed. More interestingly, she inscribed that alternation into her novels, but curiously transformed. At a number of climactic moments the play of expansion and shrinking reappears, but the rhythm is broken, lifted out of the interior life of a single character and distributed to a pair of characters, one of whom is seen expanding in loving recognition of the other, who is commonly figured as shrunken or shrinking from contact. Late in *Middlemarch,* for example, when Mrs. Bulstrode, humiliated by the revelations of her husband's past, but loyal to him nevertheless, goes to join him, we are told that "as she went towards him she thought he looked smaller—he seemed so withered and shrunken." Elsewhere in the novel, where Dorothea touches her husband's arm, only to be horrified by his unresponsive hardness, the narrator adds: "You may ask why, in the name of manliness, Mr. Casaubon should have behaved that way. Consider that this was a mind which shrank from pity."

These are instances of a distribution of attributes operating within the fictional world of the novel: images that we have seen George Eliot, in letters, applying to her own inner life are attached, as in a medieval psychomachia, to separate characters in her narratives. But at times this distributive activity may be seen operating across the boundary that separates the lives of the characters—the ways they conduct themselves and engage with one another—from the sensed activity of an author, the ways Eliot conducts the plotting of her novels. For example, Dorothea's loving acknowledgment of her husband is followed, after not too long an interval, by his death; or again, when Mrs. Bulstrode goes to her husband's side, he is a permanently broken man. Within the world of *Middlemarch*, neither Dorothea nor Mrs. Bulstrode can be held responsible for the turns of fate that crush their husbands, but it is nonetheless true that certain recipients of moral generosity don't fare well in that world. Seeking an explanation, a critic might wish to read such scenes as unwittingly playing out their author's preoccupation in some wishful and compensatory fashion. Richard Ellmann, for example, has found in the language associated with Casaubon echoes of images linked, in an early letter, with the novelists' fears of her own erotic fantasizing. "The severity with which Casaubon is treated," Ellman speculates, "would then derive from her need to exorcise this part of her experience . . . . To berate Casaubon, and to bury him, was to overcome in transformed state the narcissistic sensuality of her adolescence." To seek an author's personal allegory behind the realistic surface she has woven is often as unrewarding as it is methodologically dubious, but in the case of George Eliot's works, because they are explicitly about the imagining of others—about the status of the image of one person in the imagining mind of another—the play between the imaginer and the imagined, between author and character, and the possibility of a narcissistic confusion developing between the one and the other, has already been thematized and made available for interpretations such as Ellmann's. If anything, his claims are too modest: what he presents as a contingent psychobiographical detail—an author's uneasiness about her own "narcissism"—may be read as neither contingent nor primarily biographical, but as part of a sustained and impersonal questioning of the grounds of fiction. Nowhere is that questioning more energetically in evidence than in the pages (in chapters 20 and 21) that recount the Casaubons' experience in Rome. If we turn to them now, beginning with the final paragraphs of chapter 21, we shall find another instance of the bifurcated activity characteristic of Eliot's writing:

> Today she had begun to see that she had been under a wild illusion in expecting a response to her feeling from Mr. Casaubon,

and she had felt the waking of a presentiment that there might be a sad consciousness in his life which made as great a need on his side as on her own.

We are all of us born in moral stupidity, taking the world as an udder to feed our supreme selves: Dorothea had early begun to emerge from that stupidity, but yet it had been easier for her to imagine how she would devote herself to Mr. Casaubon, and become wise and strong in his strength and wisdom, than to conceive with that distinctness which is no longer reflection but feeling—an idea wrought back to the directness of sense, like the solidity of objects—that he had an equivalent centre of self, whence the lights and shadows must always fall with a certain difference.

These lines have been rightly admired, both as a powerful presentation of Dorothea's experience and as an epitome of the moral imagination at work, a text exhibiting the links between generous conduct, literary creation, and the reading of novels. For Dorothea's exemplary action would seem to be easily assimilated to the activity of a novelist and to that of a reader: to conceive Mr. Casaubon as different from oneself, and to do so "with that distinctness which is no longer reflection but feeling," sounds like a display of the same imaginative power that created the character of Casaubon in the first place, and the same power that *Middlemarch* would quicken in its readers. And indeed this view of the novel, and of the use of novels generally, was one that Eliot had already endorsed: "A picture of human life such as a great artist can give," she wrote, "surprises even the trivial and selfish into that attention to what is apart from themselves, which may be called the raw material of moral sentiment." We shall want to pause to ask where Mr. Casaubon fits into this set of beliefs about literature and conduct, other than as the passive (and not altogether grateful) object of Dorothea's (and Eliot's, and the reader's) regard. But first, let us look more closely at how Eliot elaborates this view of the moral imagination. The notion that literature calls attention to unnoticed aspects of life, to its intricacies or simply to its variety, is certainly not peculiar to her; more characteristic, however, is the stress she places on the reader's (or the character's) reluctance to attend: in the sentence just quoted, it is the element of surprise that counts—even "the trivial and selfish" are to be shocked into noticing what is apart from themselves. Typically her plots present someone jolted into the consciousness of others, with the jolt all the more forceful because of the resistance encountered, a resistance which is generally figured as a powerful narcissistic investment in an image of the

self, the blot that obscures the glory of the world. Or—still more generally—an investment in *some* image, for the notion of narcissism in these
novels is deepened to include other sorts of imaginative fascination.

Thus the "moral stupidity" which Dorothea must emerge from can
be presented as a clinging to a mistaken idea of her marriage: "Today she
had begun to see that she had been under a wild illusion in expecting a
response to her feeling from Mr. Casaubon." Later in the novel, echoing
the encompassing turn of phrase of the earlier passage—"We are all of us
born in moral stupidity"—Eliot writes, "We are all of us imaginative in
some form or other, for images are the brood of desire." She is writing
there of the old miser Featherstone, who never emerges or even begins to
emerge from what she names "the fellowship of illusion." But the repetitions of syntax and cadence suggest an equivalence: to be born in moral
stupidity is to be born imaginative; and it is against the inertia of this mode
of imaginative activity, the narcissistic dwelling on and in an image, that
the moral imagination has both to define itself and defend itself.

Define itself first, for the differences between these two kinds of
imagination—one supposedly turned outward and hence moral, the other
self-enclosed and narcissistic—may not, under scrutiny, be all that clear.
Both activities, whatever their outward effects, would seem to originate
within the same enclosure: it becomes important to be able to distinguish
them at their source, and not merely in terms of their consequences.
George Eliot is here engaging the same problem that led Romantic theo-
rists like Coleridge to insist on a sharp and essential difference between the
mental activities they named Imagination and Fancy, and her solution—if
we now look back at the paragraph on moral stupidity—will be seen to
resemble theirs. For what is most remarkable in that passage is the fact
that Dorothea's exemplary action, the acknowledgment of an irreducible
difference between persons, is accompanied by—is accomplished in—the
flashing reduction of another sort of difference, that between "reflection"
and "feeling," "idea" and "sense." To recognize Casaubon as possessing
"an equivalent centre of self, whence the lights and shadows must always
fall with a certain difference" is, for Dorothea, to overcome not merely
her own egotism but also what another Eliot has called a "dissociation of
sensibility," a troublesome interior difference. And, oddly, what she
achieves is made to sound very much like what Mr. Casaubon, at another
point in the novel, is pitied for having never experienced, that "rapturous
transformation of consciousness" into "the vividness of a thought, the ardour of a passion, the energy of an action." If we now ask what Mr. Casaubon is doing in this scene, we can see that he is presented both as a
character, another person, the object of Dorothea's recognition, and as a

figure, an exteriorized embodiment of a mode of imagination threaten-
ingly antithetical to hers—and to George Eliot's. For Dorothea to recognize him "as he is" is, for the author, to cast out what he may be taken to
represent.

But what, exactly, may he be taken to represent? At times he would
seem to be the personification of the written word, at others the personification of the narcissistic imagination; the connection between the two can
be made in a more systematic way in terms of an economy of anxiety, by
suggesting that the dislocation implicit in narcissism, the doubling of the
self into an eye and an image, an eye and a blot, is a more manageable and
comforting fiction than the more opening and indeterminate self-disper-
sion associated with a plurality of signs or with the plurality of interpretations that writing can provoke. In chapters 20 and 21 of *Middlemarch* one
can follow a movement toward the more reassuring fiction. They begin
with the superb paragraphs in which Mr. Casaubon is associated with a
vision of Rome as "stupendous fragmentariness," an unintelligible plurality that baffles Dorothea with "a glut of confused ideas;" they then move
through a complicated and uncertain grappling—on George Eliot's part—
with the threat of narcissism, the threat that her own imaginative activity
is nothing but narcissistic, to the exteriorization of that disturbing possibility in the figure of Casaubon, a personification now no longer of "writing" but of "narcissism" who can be "recognized" and banished from the
novel. We shall follow that movement in chapter 20 more closely in a moment, but first we should take note of some texts that bear on another
mode of imagination commonly attributed to George Eliot and held to be
at work in the paragraphs on Rome, the "historical imagination."

II

In 1856, in a review entitled "Silly Novels by Lady Novelists,"
George Eliot commented on the current vogue for historical fiction in language that reads like a program for the writing of *Romola*:

> Admitting that genius which has familiarized itself with all the
> relics of an ancient period can sometimes, by the force of its
> sympathetic divination, restore the missing notes in the "music
> of humanity," and reconstruct the fragments into a whole
> which will really bring the remote past nearer to us, and inter-
> pret it to our duller apprehension, this form of imaginative
> power must always be among the very rarest, because it de-
> mands as much accurate and minute knowledge as creative
> vigour.

Her own work on *Romola,* which she began five or six years later, involved her in months of painstaking research in reconstructing the fragments of Renaissance Florence. But the emphasis on "accurate and minute knowledge" in this passage is common to most of the essays and reviews she wrote in the 1850s, just before she turned to fiction. Knowing the names of things, getting things right becomes, for an intellectual journalist, a criterion of success and a moral criterion as well: the attention to detail required by research into any subject, but particularly into historical questions, is referred to as an escape from self, a salutary counter to the narcissism implicit in a vague and wishful relation to the things around one. Yet here a characteristic problem asserts itself: it is in the nature of historical research, even of the most rigorous and self-effacing kind, that the energies caught up in it are far from disinterested. Curiosity about the past, a wish to reconstruct the fragments into a whole, may indeed be a move beyond a casual, lazy, or provincial self-complacency, but it draws its powers from a more fundamental wish to reconstruct an original mirror of the self, a totalization of history which will be a history of one's own origins. In a bizarre scene in *Romola* George Eliot's sense of the willfulness informing attempts at historical reconstruction is dramatized in a striking and pertinent way.

Romola is both a Victorian humanist's effort to reconstruct a moment in the past and a story of a similar effort, that of the Florentine humanists, to piece together the fragments of classical civilization. One of the characters, Baldassare, is presented as someone who has been betrayed by his son into captivity and the loss of his fortune; as a result of his sufferings, we learn, he has lost his memory too, and with it his ability to read Greek. Making his way to Florence, he attempts to rehabilitate himself and to reclaim what's due him—to recapture his skills as a classical scholar and to avenge himself on his son. Eliot has constructed the plot so that these two motifs interlock in a peculiar scene. The son comes to visit Baldassare, who recognizes him and leaps at him with a dagger; but the dagger breaks, his son escapes him, and he is left alone, impotent to avenge himself and still incapable of making out the Greek text he had been puzzling over earlier:

> He leaned to take up the fragments of the dagger; then he turned towards the book which lay open at his side. It was a fine large manuscript, an odd volume of Pausanias. The moonlight was upon it, and he could see the large letters at the head of the page:

(and here George Eliot prints out the Greek capitals in a large open space on her own page before continuing):

ΜΕΣΣΝΙΚΑ. ΚΒ'

In old days he had known Pausanias familiarly; yet an hour or
two ago he had been looking hopelessly at that page, and it had
suggested no more meaning to him than if the letters had been
black weather-marks on a wall; but at this moment they were
once again the magic signs that conjure up a world.

Excitedly he takes up the book and reads, then goes out to walk about the
city, feeling "the glow of concious power":

That city, which had been a weary labyrinth, was material that
he could subdue to his purposes now: his mind glanced
through its affairs with flashing conjecture; he was once more
a man who knew cities, whose sense of vision was instructed
in large experience, who felt the keen delight of holding all
things in the grasp of language. Names! Images!—his mind
rushed through its wealth without pausing, like one who enters
on a great inheritance.

The fragments of the dagger that had failed him are replaced by the no
longer fragmentary Greek letters, once plural, discontinuous, and indeci-
pherable—mere black marks—now capable of reconstruction into a text
that is at once the mirror of Baldassare's reintegrated self (hence the excited exclamations: "Names! Images!") and the instrument of his ven-
geance. "The city, which had been a weary labyrinth"—like Casaubon's
habitual setting—is now something Baldassare can subdue to his purposes:
the mastery of language here, the reconstitution of the written word into
significant clusters, is seen as thoroughly imperialistic, an emblem of the
willed integrity of a wrathful father. There has rarely been a neater instance of what Jacques Derrida has called "ce qui revient au père": what
literally comes back to this father is his memory, his identity and with it
his power to dominate. What, then, are we to make of the historical novelist's wish to "restore the missing notes in the 'music of humanity'" and
reconstruct the fragments into a whole? That no longer sounds like an utterly innocent project. With this in mind we can now turn to the paragraphs on Rome.

III

Chapter 20 opens with Dorothea in tears, with "no distinctly shapen
grievance that she could state, even to herself." We might wish to say that
it soon becomes clear what is distressing her, that she has been hurt by her
husband's cold and pedantic behavior, and overwhelmed by what she has

seen of Rome, but that would be to travesty the experience of reading these paragraphs, to turn aside from the subtlety with which Dorothea's psychological state is rendered, as well as from the deft intermingling of the causes of her distress. From the chapter's third paragraph on, it becomes impossible to separate Dorothea's response to her husband from her response to the city, and just as impossible to allow the one noun—Casaubon—to stand in some flatly symbolic equivalence to the other noun—Rome. Certain likenesses are taken for granted: Casaubon is old, he is a historian and an interpreter, he is (to Dorothea, at least) a center of authority; but these paragraphs don't exactly dwell on this analogy or spell out its terms. Instead, the words associated earlier in the novel with Mr. Casaubon, the images that had been clustered around his name, are allowed to drift free of that center and to disperse themselves through the urban landscape: allusions to Mr. Casaubon himself, or to Dorothea's role as his wife, practically disappear. This disappearance, the withdrawal of Casaubon from the foreground of this prose, is marked by an odd figure, a sort of "dissolve" that displaces the couple's relations onto the seasons:

> Dorothea had now been five weeks in Rome, and in the kindly mornings when autumn and winter seemed to go hand in hand like a happy aged couple one of whom would presently survive in chiller loneliness, she had driven about at first with Mr. Casaubon, but of late chiefly with Tantripp and their experienced courier.

While Mr. Casaubon retires to the Vatican Library, Dorothea is left alone with Rome and her own life, and both are figured to her as enigmas: her confused and disorganized feelings are assimilated to the fragmentary nature of the scene around her, a scene now made up as much of the bits and pieces of language associated with Casaubon as of the "broken revelations of that Imperial and Papal city":

> The weight of unintelligible Rome might lie easily on bright nymphs to whom it formed a background for the brilliant picnic of Anglo-foreign society; but Dorothea had no such defence against deep impressions. Ruins and basilicas, palaces and colossi, set in the midst of a sordid present, where all that was living and warm-blooded seemed sunk in the deep degeneracy of a superstition divorced from reverence; the dimmer yet eager Titantic life gazing and struggling on walls and ceilings; the long vistas of white forms whose marble eyes seemed to hold the monotonous light of an alien world: all this vast wreck of

ambitious ideals, sensuous and spiritual, mixed confusedly with signs of breathing forgetfulness and degradation, at first jarred her with an electric shock, and then urged themselves on her with that ache belonging to a glut of confused ideas which check the flow of emotion. Forms both pale and glowing took possession of her young sense, and fixed themselves in her memory even when she was not thinking of them, preparing strange associations which remained through her after-years. Our moods are apt to bring with them images which succeed each other like the magic-lantern pictures of a doze; and in certain states of dull forlornness Dorothea all her life continued to see the vastness of St. Peter's, the huge bronze canopy, the excited intention in the attitudes and garments of the prophets and evangelists in the mosaics above, and the red drapery which was being hung for Christmas spreading itself everywhere like a disease of the retina.

I have quoted this passage at length both in order to recall its intensity and to draw attention to its organization. The persistent emphasis on the scene's at once soliciting and resisting comprehension, linked to the rhythms in which these sentences accumulate layer on layer of plural nouns, until that accumulated charge is released in a "shock," a "glut of confused ideas which check the flow of emotion"—these elements mark Dorothea's experience as an experience of the sublime, in the specific sense that term took on in the writings of Kant or Wordsworth. I mention this not simply to identify a literary tradition—though I have enough of Casaubon in me to take an intense, bleak pleasure in interrupting a passionate moment with a scholarly gloss—but because to recognize the rhythm of the sublime in these sentences is to anticipate where the text might go from here, what one might expect to follow after that abrupt shock. At one point, for instance, Kant describes the feeling of the sublime as a pleasure that arises only indirectly, produced "by the feeling of a momentary checking of the vital powers and a consequent stronger outflow of them." Elsewhere, explaining the "bewilderment or, as it were, perplexity which it is said seizes the spectator on his first entrance into St. Peter's in Rome," he writes: "For there is here a feeling of the inadequacy of his imagination for presenting the ideas of a whole, wherein the imagination reaches its maximum, and, in striving to surpass it, sinks back into itself, by which, however, a kind of emotional satisfaction is produced." We might, with this model in mind, ask if there will be an outflow of vital powers in this passage or a sinking back of the imagination into itself. Or, if what we have in mind is the language of "Tintern Abbey," we might wonder if Dorothea will be released from "the burthen of the mystery," the "heavy and the weary weight of all this unintelligible world," and allowed to "see into the life of things." One way or another, a reader may be led to expect some resolution, and, indeed, these expectations are rewarded, although— and this too is characteristic of the sublime—not in quite the form antici- pated.

For the movement of these pages seems to issue in not one but three moments that qualify as "resolutions," partly because of their position in the text, partly because of the level of their diction and the nature of the metaphors of which they are composed. One of these, the last in the se- quence, I have already described in some detail: it is the paragraph with which chapter 21 concludes, the paragraph beginning "We are all of us born in moral stupidity." For if it is the "dream-like strangeness of her bridal life" that Dorothea is confronting in the opening pages of chapter 20, the baffling disparity between her sense of whom she was marrying and the realities of living with Mr. Casaubon, then her acknowledging that she had "been under a wild illusion" can be thought of as one re- sponse to the shock she registered in the previous chapter, a response that is deferred chiefly for reasons of dramatic verisimilitude, because it takes time to adjust to such new awareness. Here the sequence of sublime check- ing followed by some resolution underlies the ethical scenario we noticed earlier, where a character is jolted out of moral stupidity into the recogni- tion of something apart from the self.

But the intensity of Dorothea's feelings, as they are presented in these opening paragraphs, as well as the scope of Eliot's rhetoric, are far in ex- cess of anything that could be resolved dramatically: she has been shown attempting to come to terms not simply with her husband, but with the heterogeneous assault of Rome, with a collection of signs that may be summed up in a verbal formulation (e.g. "all this vast wreck of ambitious ideals") but which neither Dorothea nor the author is in a position to render as a totality. The resolution of *this* aspect of Dorothea's experience is to be found in the sentences immediately following those on the check- ing of the flow of emotion, and in one sense it is no resolution at all: it takes the form of a compulsively repeated set of images, fixed in Doro- thea's memory for life and unexorcisable. The plurality of unmasterable fragments is converted into a repetitive series of painful tokens. This is a dark sublimity, beyond the pleasure principle for Dorothea, and suffi- ciently at odds with the values of Victorian humanism to be distressing to

George Eliot as well. The later paragraph, in which Dorothea recognizes Casaubon, may be read as, quite literally, a domestication of the anxiety associated with the earlier moment.

If one wanted to demonstrate that *Middlemarch* offers a reader two incompatible systems of value, conflicting views of the interpretation of history, of the possibilities of knowledge, of the consistency of the self, few passages in the novel would provide better evidence. One could contrast the sublime of repetition with that of recognition, then read the first as an undermining of moral and metaphysical categories, the second as the recuperation of those same categories. But what, then, are we to make of still another moment in these pages that is bound to strike a reader as "sublime"? It is to be found in the paragraph immediately following the description of Rome, and it has been cited, admiringly, perhaps as much as any other passage in Eliot's works:

> If we had a keen vision and a feeling for all ordinary human life, it would be like hearing the grass grow and the squirrel's heart beat, and we should die of that roar which lies on the other side of silence. As it is the quickest of us walk about well wadded in stupidity.

We might begin by noticing that these sentences, although they share with the other "resolutions" a sense of high-powered epistemological confrontation, are not about Dorothea's response either to Rome or to Mr. Casaubon; they are, rather, about how "we"—the readers and the narrator—might respond to Dorothea, and indeed they come at the end of a paragraph that had begun with a slightly awkward wavering of tone, as the narrator seemed to back off from the intensities of Dorothea's experience:

> Not that this inward amazement of Dorothea's was anything very exceptional: many souls in their young nudity are tumbled out among incongruities and left to "find their feet" among them, while their elders go about their business. Nor can I suppose that when Mrs. Casaubon is discovered in a fit of weeping six weeks after her wedding the situation will be regarded as tragic.

One of Eliot's most acute contemporary readers, Richard Holt Hutton, was struck by the oddness of these lines, and bothered by what he heard as a "bitter parenthetical laugh" at the expense of those souls tumbled out "in their young nudity" I think it *is* an odd moment, but that the tonal irony seems less directed at the "souls"—that is, at Dorothea—than it does at some imagined insensitive reader: the "Nor can I suppose" is somewhat heavyhandedly reminding her readers of their perception of the tragic, of the limits of those powers of sympathetic imagination which would enable them to discern the tragic in "the very fact of frequency." Still more puzzling, however, is the combination of this sardonic diction with the note of high assurance the narrator strikes in the sentences about "the roar . . . on the other side of silence."

What is going on in this passage makes more sense once we learn that it is dense with self-quotation, with allusions to George Eliot's earlier fiction. Those "souls in their young nudity," for example, "tumbled out" and left to "find their feet" would seem to be a rendering as a figure of speech of what was once, in a story called "Janet's Repentance" (one of the *Scenes of Clerical Life*), a piece of dramatic action: there the heroine is literally thrown out of her house by her drunken husband, and her situation is described in these terms:

> The stony street, the bitter north-east wind and darkness—and in the midst of them a tender woman thrust out from her husband's home in her thin night-dress, the harsh wind cutting her naked feet, and driving her long hair away from her half-clad bosom, where the poor heart is crushed with anguish and despair.

Also to be found in "Janet's Repentance" are lines which echo in the squirrel's heartbeat:

> Yet surely, surely the only true knowledge of our fellow-man is that which enables us to feel with him—which gives us a fine ear for the heart-pulses that are beating under the mere clothes of circumstance and opinion. Our subtlest analysis of schools and sects must miss the essential truth, unless it be lit up by the love that sees in all forms of human thought and work the life and death struggles of separate human beings.

In still another story, "The Lifted Veil," the hero discovers in himself a power that torments him and which he describes as a "diseased participation in other people's consciousness": "It was like a preternaturally heightened sense of hearing," he relates, "making audible to one a roar of sound where others find perfect stillness."

The validity of the novelist's imagination of others, whether it is seen as a saving gift or as a curse, is what is at stake in the lines on the squirrel's heartbeat. Placed between Dorothea's failure to reconstruct the fragments of history and her success in recognizing her husband as someone with an "equivalent centre of self," this passage seeks language adequate to a slightly different task, that of stabilizing the incommensurable relation between an author conceived of as somehow "outside" (but uncertainly outside) her creation and a privileged (but fictitious) consciousness within that imagined world. The allusions to earlier works of fiction, the reappearance of those evocations of pathos or of imaginative power, are accompanied by the reversal of their original meanings: what had seemed pathetic reality in "Janet's Repentance" has been transformed into a metaphor, and the "fine ear for heart-pulses," the ability to hear "a roar of sound where others find perfect stillness"—these are precisely the faculties that a reader is now told he does not possess. The wavering, then steadying of tone in which the narrator addresses the reader may be read as one way of readjusting to the felt instability of the author's relation to her character, to the unsettled sense that it was through an intense identification with Dorothea's experience in Rome that the magnificent previous paragraph had been written, but that the burden of that paragraph was the fictitiousness and the willfulness of such identifications. The sublimity of the image of the roar on the other side of silence emerges from this thoroughly negative insight.

Behind this language about the limits of perception is still another text, one with a long history in eighteenth- and nineteenth-century writing about the sublime: it is the passage in the *Essay Concerning Human Understanding* in which Locke praises the aptness with which the human senses are scaled to man's position in the hierarchy of creatures:

If our sense of hearing were but a thousand times quicker than it is, how would a perpetual noise distract us. And we should in the quietest retirement be less able to sleep or meditate than in the middle of a sea-fight. Nay, if that most instructive of senses, seeing, were in any man a thousand, or a hundred thousand times more acute than it is by the best microscope, things several millions of times less than the smallest object of his sight now would then be visible to his naked eyes, and so he would come nearer to the discovery of the texture and motion of the minute parts of corporeal things: and in many of them, probably get ideas of their internal constitutions; but then he would be in a quite different world from other people: nothing would appear the same to him and others.

Locke's language converts a scaled continuum into an oppostion between the ordinary world of sensation and sociability and the "quite different world" in which the man with microscopic vision would find himself. To allude to that language in *Middlemarch* is to stress that particular discontinuity at the moment when the incommensurability between an author and the creatures of her pen is under consideration. Suppose, to draw out the turns of this figure, one *were* to hear the roar which lies on the other side of silence. Possibly one might not die of it; instead—and this may not be the preferable alternative—one might become like Locke's man, moving nearer to the discovery of the texture and motion of things, but in a quite different world from other people. If, for example, one were to bring a drop of Mr. Casaubon's blood into focus, one might see nothing but semicolons and parentheses. That is the possibility that is written into *Middlemarch* in the idiom of the sublime; it is clearly not a possibility to be steadily contemplated by a working novelist—it must be repressed if books like *Middlemarch* are to be written at all. One sign of that repression is the recognition and exorcism of Casaubon.

Origins, *Middlemarch*, Endings: George Eliot's Crisis of the Antecedent

Jan B. Gordon

> *What was the primitive tissue? In that way Lydgate put the question—not quite in the way required by the awaiting answer; but such missing of the right word befalls many seekers.*
>
> (chap. 15)

Lydgate joins a number of *Middlemarch* residents who attempt to locate a single point of Origin from whence reform—political, physiological, ontological, fictional—might be understood to have begun. His quest for the primitive tissue, Casaubon's circuitous search for a Key to All Mythologies, Ladislaw's infatuation with the pre Pre-Raphaelite art of the Nazarenes, even George Eliot's setting the novel "back" to the eve of the First Reform Bill all testify to an ardent willingness to believe in some pure Origin of events prior to the corruption by "circumstances" that transform those obsessions to an interest in mere Endings. This imagined Origin was to be sure a fixation of the Victorian mind with its fascination for tracing various lines of succession, whether it be Darwin's *Origin of Species*, Newman's apostolic succession, remounted in order to discover some presumably original Church, or the project to compile an *Oxford English Dictionary* that would trace the lineaments of linguistic origin and descent. The very figure of the orphan itself, as J. Hillis Miller has argued, bespeaks an interest in the fear of discontinuity which prompts so many of the age's novel-

---

From *George Eliot: Centenary Essays and an Unpublished Fragment*, edited by Anne Smith. © 1980 by Vision Press Ltd.

istic children to commence the pilgrimage that might bring them into some confrontation with their Origin-as-parent. The Victorian orphan figure can typically make his vocational choice only after he has ascertained his private history, which is but another way of saying that he is his Origin. He goes through life under the assumption that the structure of the journey is dependent upon the clarification of his point of departure. Conceived of in such a manner, the Origin is never transitive insofar as it has no object other than its continual clarification. Its model is self-consciousness. Ever so gradually, however, the awful truth emerges: that Origins, "Keys," primitive tissues, sources, historical "background"—the Urtexts of an epoch—are arbitrary and fictional rather than real, mere attempts to individually appropriate that metaphysical absence which is every Origin.

Those motivated by the quest for some identifiable Origin at the outset of *Middlemarch* tend to share a similar metaphoric world. Perhaps its most salient characteristic is a belief that any source embodies a wholeness and purity which is fragmented and refracted in all descendants. For Casaubon, "the genuine mythical product" has a purity diluted by the "fable of Cupid and Psyche" (chap. 20) which he sees as only a mere romantic invention, i.e. corruption. And the difficulty is that of somehow getting beyond the various corruptions, filling those interstices which separate the scholar from truth. The world appears as a cluster of fragments which simultaneously obscures yet reveals some originally "given" condition, a prior status. And, in order to enforce any *a priori* wholeness, Casaubon must multiply their fragmented nature "made difficult by the interference of citations, or by the rivalry of dialectical phrases ringing against each other in his brain" (chap. 29) in order to assure himself of the presence of sufficient "evidence." His is the unenviable psychological position of having to create obstructive refractions in order that the true light might appear brighter. Revelation and distancing are mutually reenforcing, producing an incredible circularity rather than any origin which might serve as a commencement.

Hence the predominance and significance of the water imagery which Reva Stump has so carefully catalogued; in order to find the elusive Key to All Mythologies, Casaubon must get beyond the tributaries of knowledge, those shallow rivers where lurk Carp, Pike and Trench, and into the clearer reservoirs which they share as a common source of life. The irony of Casaubon's plight lies in the fact that, although he thinks himself on some tortuous journey of connection, his own language reveals symptoms of a discontinuity that belies his life's purpose. Mrs. Cadwallader's judgement that he is "all semicolons and parentheses" (chap. 8) seems borne out by his circuitous marriage proposal. In order to create the illusion of connection, he must rely upon the verbal reservoirs of parenthetical expression that force us to lose sight of any Origin:

> For in the first hour of meeting you, I had an impression of your eminent and perhaps exclusive fitness to supply that need (connected, I may say, with such activity of the affections as even the preoccupations of a work too special to be abdicated could not uninterruptedly dissimulate); and each succeeding opportunity for observation has given the impression an added depth by convincing me more emphatically of that fitness.
>
> (chap. 5)

Even as he tries to arrive at an Ending (the proposal), he betrays "need" as an Origin which replicates itself as connective "successions." Given his perception of the relation between a shared ontic Origin and the descent of myth into the mass of *parergae,* Casaubon's language has its own logic. He either overwrites in order to fill in all gaps so as to create his own meaning at the core of a linguistic labyrinth or, conversely, he underwrites, using a kind of shorthand to point to the metaphysical truth which he assumes to lie beyond the visible. For example, he never refers to content, but only dates in summarizing previous correspondence, convinced that a "*vide supra* could serve instead of a repetition" (chap. 3). He is always at pains to make clear to Dorothea the nature of "received" opinion during their honeymoon in Rome, as if the meaning of history were present in the footprints of the cognoscenti.

To be sure, such assumptions have a puritan bias. If all truth is revealed, then existence in the ordinary world centres about locating the identifying fragmentary "evidence" so that all objects and opinions eventually come to assume the status of clues. But, simultaneously, such a conviction entails a corollary belief that "all the mythical systems or erratic mythical fragments in the world were corruptions of a tradition originally revealed" (chap. 3). Little wonder that a phenomenology of the "clue" eventually brings Casaubon to a suspicion of human as well as object infidelity. For Casaubon the world is a corrupted text, and his every effort is restorative insofar as it attempts to locate some single authority which lies behind the multiplicity of meanings and systems. In one sense, what Casaubon does do is to make a distinction between a primary source and secondary literature, or between a unified Original and its limitations. Such is the space in which traditional hermeneutics operates and depends for its efficacy upon the closed and hence "sacred" nature of the Origin. As the nineteenth century applied interpretation to scripture in order to consider

it as a mode of fiction, so Casaubon applies hermeneutics to fictions in order to restore the difference between an Origin and a lapsed text! When in
chapter 22 Ladislaw reminds us that Casaubon, unlike the German, Ot-
fried Muller, "is not an Orientalist," he is pointing out the futility of the
effort. Muller's *Prolegomena to a Scientific Mythology*, published in 1825, had
ruled out the so-called etymological proofs that had attempted to relate diverse myths to a common Hebrew origin by showing conclusively that
mythologies develop independently and arbitrarily, to serve the totemic
needs of different societies. Unlike her Casaubon who reads no German,
George Eliot knew of Muller's research, having mentioned it in her review
of R. W. Mackay's *The Progress of the Intellect* in the *Westminster Review* of
January 1851. Perhaps as a consequence of this inability to resolve the
many into the One, Casaubon exhibits other rigidly puritan behavioural
attitudes. If he is not engaging life (spending) and also getting no nearer
the goal (quest achievement), then it follows that Casaubon must be "saving." He comes to believe that "his long studious bachelorhood had stored
up for him a compound interest of enjoyment" (chap. 10). It is but another
reservoir in his life, waiting to be tapped. Such is a life lived totally in the
conditional; that is to say that Casaubon, like so many Middlemarchers,
comes to believe that one decision, one act, will make him. And, as Fred
Vincy with old Featherstone's will, only then will he begin to "live." Such
a dynamics of dependency, as we shall see, instantly converts life to a gamble that feeds postponement.

Dorothea, somewhat similarly, creates in Casaubon an Origin out of
an absence:

> Dorothea's faith supplied all that Mr. Casaubon's words
> seemed to leave unsaid; what believer sees a disturbing omis-
> sion or infelicity? The text, whether of prophet or poet, ex-
> pands for whatever we can put into it, and even his bad gram-
> mar is sublime.
>
> (chap. 5)

Just as Casaubon's shorthand involves the use of "touchstones" of criti-
cally respectable opinion, so Dorothea somewhat similarly begins to see
emptiness—Casaubon's deep-set eyes, for example—as signs which point
beyond themselves. She, too, is compelled to create continuities out of the
obviously discontinuous. Paralleling Casaubon's attempt to posit the cate-
gory of the *subauditum* to account for a missing word from the text of the
quotation of some French king in chapter 9, Dorothea

> filled up all blanks with unmanifested perfections, interpret-
> ing him as she interpreted the works of Providence, and ac-

counting for seeming discords by her own deafness to the higher harmonies.

The Origin always embodies *harmony* for those who believe in it; reconciling all differences, it lies behind the proliferation of refracted signs in the universe at large. Hence Casaubon represents a combination of "religious elevation" and "learning":

> here was a living Bossuet, whose work would reconcile complete knowledge with devoted piety; he was a modern Augustine who united the glories of doctor and saint.
>
> (chap. 3)

Like every Origin, he is a tautology, "a man whose learning almost amounted to a proof of whatever he believed" (chap. 2). The same Dorothea who in the famous discussion with her sister Celia over the family jewels, came to regard gems as "fragments of heaven," conceives of herself as a fragmented text who must learn Hebrew, "at least the alphabet and a few roots—in order to arrive at the core of things" (chap. 7). Casaubon's logocentric universe is replaced in Dorothea's thought by Casaubon himself who "thinks a whole world of which my thought is but a poor two-penny mirror" (chap. 3).

Hence, one of the predominant strains of imagery in the early chapters of the novel: those on a quest for Origins want *illumination* which must come from some source outside themselves. If the acolyte inhabits the naves of cognitive shadows and reflections, the Origin must be illuminated Unity. The artificial distinction manifests itself in a psychological chiaroscuro. Dorothea is often seen in relief against some background that looms large and which places her, from one point of view at least, in the shadows of an historical epic frieze. It is not merely that the novel's first sentence introduces us to a woman "whose beauty seems to be thrown into relief by poor dress," but also that the gloom of Lowick "had no bloom that could be thrown into relief by that background" (chap. 9). The realm of relief or fresco is part of the world of assumed antithesis which recognizes a distinction between foreground and background, both historical and aesthetic. Perhaps its most ironic commentator is Naumann, the Nazarene painter whom the Casaubons meet in Rome. Clad in her Quakerish grey drapery with long cloak and ungloved hand, Dorothea is in the attitude of some historical bas-relief, awaiting illumination. Her presence in the museum creates a juxtaposition which appeals to those who wish to use the "here" only as a vehicle for gaining access to the "there" of historical antecedent:

> There lies antique beauty, not corpse-like even in death, but arrested in the complete contentment of its sensuous perfection: and here stands beauty in its breathing life, with the consciousness of Christian centuries in its bosom.
>
> (chap. 19)

The Naumanns of the world of course see the contrasts for what they are—opportunities for caricatures, seized when he uses Casaubon's head as the model for St. Thomas Aquinas. Whereas so many of the other characters search for an historical model that lies back of and behind the corrupted "texts," Naumann arbitrarily uses the "living" Casaubon as a model for the historical St. Thomas, creating a mock-relief in the process of substitution. Conversely, moments of real moral illumination in the novel are invariably the consequence of some deadening in historical contrast. Following her return from the honeymoon in Rome, "each remembered thing in the room was disenchanted, was deadened as an unlit transparency" (chap. 28). Chiaroscuro tends to diminish in *Middlemarch* at those moments when an individual comes to recognize that "sources" do not always reveal connection, but are organizational fictions. At the outset, every dwelling in *Middlemarch* seems to ooze with a contrast between the shallowed dimensionality of present objects and some deeper set background, represented best perhaps in Farebrother's parsonage where the "standing in relief against the dark wainscot" present a unique physiognomy (chap. 17). The spatial algebra of historical consciousness—background is to foreground as Origin is to descent, providing illumination, enchantment and obsession as the common denominator—is violated upon the discovery that the Origin can also be an imaginative corruption. It is Ladislaw, as we would expect, who first thinks to himself, in one of the novel's great puns: "She must have made some original romance for herself in this marriage" (chap. 21).

Lydgate too compensates for his own obscure Origins by an obsession with locating some Ur-tissue that might explain the various systemic functions which seem to be independent:

> it was open to another mind to say, have not these structures some *common basis* from which they have all started, as your sarsnet, gauze, net, satin and velvet from the raw cocoon? Here would be another light, as of oxy-hydrogen, showing the very grain of things, and revising all former explanations. Of this *sequence* to Bichat's work . . . Lydgate was enamoured.
>
> (chap. 15)

A "common basis" which lies behind some "sequence" implies the necessity of locating some missing link, "new connections and hitherto hidden facts of structure which must be taken into account in considering the symptoms of maladies and the action of medicaments" (chap. 15). Lydgate's idol, the Frenchman Bichat, demarcated one of the nineteenth century's most famous medical cul-de-sacs by positing a "primary tissue," a sort of cellular phlogiston, from which various organs were descended. As Casaubon's researches lead to the construction of compartmentalized boxes of notes, beginning with the first letter of the alphabet and as George Eliot herself had commenced a novel with the first two letters of the alphabet in the process of creating an emotional Adamic everyman, so Lydgate's career begins at the beginning. He takes from its shelf the first volume of an encyclopedia and becomes enamoured with the entries under "Anatomy." The portals which opened upon Dorothea's marriage—"everything he had said seemed like a specimen from a mine, or the inscription on the door of a museum" (chap. 3)—are translated into Lydgate's *valvae,* the portals of the human heart, which first attract his attention.

The remainder of his life becomes devoted to "filling the vast spaces" (chap. 15) which lie between himself and the great originators, the science of first things. Perhaps the most poignant feature of Lydgate's plight is his attempt to break away from an Origins-dominated world view. He becomes early smitten with an interest in "structure," investigating the nervous system with the aid of galvanic experiments. But what neither he nor Casaubon nor Dorothea can ever do is to acknowledge the possibility of either a divided source or conflicting motives. Discontinuity of development is simply not broached as a possibility, and it is for precisely this reason that Lydgate is so disillusioned by the Madame Laure episode. Her foot really slipped, but she "meant to do it" (chap. 15) suggests a conflict between motive and action rather than some commonly shared source. Again, with Lydgate, there is the pull of postponement; like Casaubon's delayed "beginning," Lydgate sees marriage as impetuous if not removed to "some distant period." It is almost as if some conservation of absence were at work here—as if the desire to fill some gap which separates the discoverer from an origin shifts that gap to the end of the sequence, delaying Endings. The isolation in some "middle" creates a self-induced wager:

> He was at a starting-point which makes many a man's career a
> fine subject for betting if there were any gentlemen given to
> that amusement.
>
> (chap. 15)

The physical embodiment of that "long shot" is Fred Vincy, for his life can begin only when he is "made" by Featherstone's will. And it is that absent bequest—the non-materialized Origin—which prompts the speculation that leads to his indebtedness. In one sense he hypostasizes an unknown Origin as collateral, a displacement common in the social dynamics of *Middlemarch*. And when he is forced to deny such speculation, old Featherstone asks him to contradict the story by bringing proof in the form of documents which become a substitute for authority:

> "But I contradict it again. The story is a silly lie."
> "Nonsense! you must bring dockiments. It comes from authority."

> (chap. 12)

Like all the other people who regard authority, origins, and text synonymously, Fred Vincy is asked to collect proof in the form of a written statement. His "dockiments" would presumably join Mr. Brooke's pre-campaign trail ammunition, "his documents on machine-breaking and rick-burning" (chap. 3) piled in a heap in a study which forms an "authoritative" base for later claims:

> "Yes," said Mr. Brooke, with an easy smile, "but I have documents. I began a long while ago to collect documents. They want arranging, but when a question has struck me, I have written to somebody and got an answer. I have documents at my back. But now, how do you arrange your documents?"
> "In pigeon-holes partly," said Mr. Casaubon, with rather a startled air of effort.

> (chap. 2)

One of the ways of measuring the change that comes over the Middlemarch community during the course of the novel is the shift in the symbolic status of documents. Early in the novel documents are regarded as sources of authority, the means by which some proof is accumulated or evidence is acquired. Documents are always "fragments" of some larger tapestry and hence always point beyond themselves. They tend to have synecdochic value insofar as the various scraps of paper represent, if correctly arranged and sifted, some larger truth. It is in such a light that Casaubon arranges his notes in compartments and that Fred Vincy is requested to furnish proof that he has not speculated, the irony lying of course in the fact that a piece of paper is to be used to ascertain a *negative* involvement. What he is really being asked to do is to document a lack of proof, the same task at which Casaubon has been labouring for years. And Casaubon's will possesses the same symmetry, really; it is not a bequest but a negative injunction, providing *no* inheritance upon the fulfilment of certain conditions. The codicil is another "authority" suggesting Casaubon's lack of authority! Stated in another way, the documents become, quite arbitrarily, part of the burden of guilt disguised as bequests. Casaubon's will has a fictional, creative base, since it *creates* suspicion rather than authorizes distribution. Perhaps the best example of all in the novel is old Featherstone's will, upon which Fred Vincy has staked so much. The diminishment of this particular "beginning" for Fred is surely signalled by the existence of one will behind another. His point of Origin is part of a sequence of infinite regress, and not some commencement of a delayed life. Even were Mary Garth to obey Featherstone's final request, she still would not know which will had priority, for the two wills cancel each other. She has no power to act, and he has no real power to authorize. In the beginning is a binary set that is arbitrarily established and not a communally shared Origin from which benefits flow, the "homogenous origin of all the tissues" (chap. 45) which Lydgate has posited.

Gradually, those who draw up documents in *Middlemarch* became conscious of their ultimate arbitrariness. After Casaubon's death Dorothea occupies herself with maps and papers relating to Lowick, the pragmatic accoutrements by which we set our affairs in order:

> One morning, about eleven, Dorothea was seated in her boudoir with a map of the land attached to the manor and other papers before her, which were to help her in making an *exact statement for herself* of her income and affairs.
>
> (chap. 54)

This event takes place immediately after she has sealed and put in a drawer forever one of the last instructional documents of her late husband, a "Synoptical Tabulation for the use of Mrs. Casaubon," one of the cornerstones of Casaubon's imaginary scholarly edifice. Both documents are tabulations, but Dorothea is now willing to acknowledge, at least passively, that all inventories have the self and not the world as the unstated recipient. It is part of a shift in the status of texts, part of the change from envisioning the document as *fragment* to seeing it instead as part of an arbitrary *collection* whose object is the self.

Fragments have a phenomenology that implies descent from some prior status of wholeness, and in *Middlemarch* they tend to accumulate about those people whose mission it is to prove that the many stem from some One. Fragments are adjuncts to the telos of reform and have an historical component precisely to the extent that some cataclysm in time separates *them* from *it*. In Levi-Strauss's nomenclature the fragment might be imagined to be nature striving to be culture. The danger which threatens those obsessed with the document-as-fragment lies in the fact that it is too often made to do more than its nature will allow:

> "That is fine, Ladislaw: that is the way to put it. Write that down, now. We must begin to get documents about the feeling of the country, as well as the machine-breaking and general distress."
>
> "As to documents," said Will, "a two-inch card will hold plenty. A few rows of figures are enough to deduce misery from."
>
> (chap. 46)

The aim here is to deduce a common source in human emotion for the "feelings" which are somehow represented in figures. Brooke is enlisting the restless Ladislaw in yet another of those quests for homogeneity. What is at stake of course is a gross misunderstanding of the nature of the deductive process. There is no single source for either human authority or human misery, any more than Rome, that city of fragments, as Dorothea discovers on her honeymoon, illuminates historical consciousness. It is rather more rightly understood as the "interpreter of the world" (chap. 20) which suggests the possibility of other interpretations. Everyone's language is unique unto himself. The decline of any conviction in a "source" is manifested as the democratization of the vernacular:

> "Are you beginning to dislike slang, then?" said Rosamond, with mild gravity.
>
> "Only the wrong sort. All choice of words is slang. It marks a class."
>
> (chap. 11)

When Fred Vincy recognizes that he can no longer depend upon Featherstone's will, but must instead learn how to keep the clerk's memoranda at Caleb Garth's warehouse, he must literally learn how to write anew: not the scholarly manuscript of the would-be cleric—"easy to interpret when you *know beforehand* what the writer means" (chap. 56)—but the transactional style that depends less upon an understanding of origin or intention:

> "Now, Fred," said Caleb, "you will have some desk-work.
> I have always done a good deal of writing myself, and I can't

do without help, and as I want you to understand the accounts and get the values into your head, I mean to do without another clerk. So you must buckle to. How are you at writing and arithmetic?"

(chap. 56)

He is among those who must keep records, not in order to construct a proof, but to transmit arbitrary information whose independent components have a more or less equal status. Fred's work comes to assume the characteristics of Mary's hobby, "copying the labels from a heap of shallow cabinet drawers in a minute handwriting" (chap. 57) or Dorothea's compulsive desire to write out "her memoranda" to the housekeeper whenever Will drops in (chap. 62). Like Will's own portfolio, all of these documents are not fragments at all, but arbitrary collections without any potential for internal development and lacking a clearly defined beginning or ending other than the arbitrary. These are the "circumstances" toward which texts accrue in *Middlemarch*. Lydgate's list of household furnishings drawn up for his creditors and Bulstrode's "pocket-book to review various memoranda there as to the arrangements he had projected and partly carried out in the prospect of quitting Middlemarch" (chap. 70) are contingency texts, preparations for possibilities rather than steps in a proof. Like Rosamond's invitation lists, these collections of documents, bills, memoranda, and lists have value only as exchange. They facilitate social transaction, but have no worth outside their denotative systems. Such are "service papers" which authenticate social intercourse; they do not form a part of what George Eliot calls in one place "geognosis."

The character in the novel who first recognizes this distinction is Farebrother, whose insect collection, unlike Casaubon's pigeon-holes, has only a private value within a system of potential exchange. His "old texts" (chap. 17) include items about a variety "of Aphis brassicae," or a learned treatise on the "entomology of the Pentateuch" (chap. 17) which has fictional status only:

"I have some sea-mice—fine specimens—in spirits. And I will throw in Robert Brown's new thing—*Microscopic Observations on the Pollen of Plants*—if you don't happen to have it already."

"Why, seeing how you long for the monster, I might ask a higher price. Suppose I ask you to look through my drawers and agree with me about all my new species?"

(chap. 17)

Farebrother's collection is almost a parody of the research into Origins that characterizes the would-be discoverers in *Middlemarch*. The curator of specimens rather than fragments, he alone recognizes that his fascination with what he calls "natural history" is private insofar as it is likely to reveal much more about himself than about any lineage in the animal kingdom. His is simply an insect collection in which one specimen is the equivalent of any other, except during exchange. They can be arranged into an almost infinite number of communities, including an imaginary parliament. Unlike the other clerics and exemplars of piety in the novel, he lacks a text, always electing to deliver his sermons "without a book" (chap. 18). Rather than looking for the general law which is supposed to lie behind random events in the universe, Farebrother alone is aware that the individual imposes himself upon any formulation in an activity akin to translation. Everyman his own anthropomorphist is a sentiment surely relevant to the translator of Feuerbach. Farebrother it is who always reminds us of the dangers which stem from mistaking the convenience of an interpretation for the status of an Original that demands obligations; contrasting himself with Bulstrode, Farebrother reminds Lydgate: "I don't *translate* my own convenience into other people's duties" (chap. 17, italics mine). The problem in *Middlemarch* is that systems of exchange and substitution which are essentially horizontal are continually making claims which presume vertical priorities in such a way that the discontinuous is never acknowledged.

Farebrother is clearly a man of "endings," for the Vicar loves to play at cards with the hopes of winning those small sums that make life easier:

> The vicar was a first-rate billiard-player, and, though he did
> not frequent the Green Dragon, there were reports that he had
> sometimes been there in the daytime and had won money.
>
> (chap. 18)

Although his friends regard Farebrother's casual card games and billiard-playing as "ignoble," the Vicar is clearly distinguished by his love of games as opposed to myths. The money "had never been a motive to him" but rather the physical translation of winning or losing. His approach to gambling, because it is so motiveless, is in direct contrast to those in the community who are always attempting to secure the metaphoric windfall that will make their postponements worthwhile. Their motivation is perhaps best seen, in terms of George Eliot's crisis of the antecedent, as the urge to recovery, and such urges participate in the structural pattern of the labyrinth.

As the imagined Origin retreats into the distance, the researchers in

Middlemarch, in contrast to Ladislaw or Farebrother, recognize that they have paid an enormous price. Neither Casaubon, nor Lydgate, nor Dorothea see any tangible return on their investment. Every potential fulfilment becomes part of a vague future; such is the martyrdom of the ardent. The sacrifice consists of neutralizing the present in favour of a gamble upon the future benefits, and when that reward becomes illusory, life assumes the dynamics of an enormous risk. One consequence of this risk is a kind of speculation which creates its own centre out of nothingness. Fred's speculation upon the horse which he does not own; Casaubon's will, a mode of borrowing time posthumously; Lydgate's borrowings to purchase the household goods for his marriage; and Bulstrode's too easy acquiescence to Raffles's threat of blackmail, in effect giving the banker a rented past, are all desperate gambles by which the gambler attempts either to blot out the past (erasing the gap which separates him from Origins) or, conversely, to bring the condition of windfall from the future to the present. In either case, from a structural point of view, gambling is part of the dynamics of an "expanded middle."

All of this activity comes under the general rubric of speculation, part of the new mercantilism that intrudes upon an older, more traditional historical consciousness in the novel. But the implications of this gambling in which all of those engaged in the quest for Origins find themselves involved, suggests something larger. It is not merely that men named Rigg and Raffles come to have such an important bearing on the action of the novel. But rather that increasing ontological risk would appear to be a corollary to the decline of traditional authority. What Fred Vincy does, in effect, is to make Fate his authority rather than Featherstone by creating an infinite sequence of dependencies, with one horse becoming collateral for another. Such a world resembles that of Lydgate where he uses that which he does not own—a successful practice—as the basis for borrowing against the future. Casaubon does the same, negatively, in the codicil to his will: he speculates by putting his money on Dorothea's future at the moment when he has no future! The structure of the risk is worthy of note, because it tends to shift the pattern of infinite regress, which had been imagined to be in the past by those who quest for Origins, into future time.

Additionally, the act of gambling tends to neutralize those objects which provide the basis for the speculation. To put up "stakes" is one way of saying that one does not own the object, but is instead willing to play for it. Edmund Bergler suggests that gambling is a highly symbolic activity where the items wagered are less significant *per se* than they are as part of a larger system with its own language that is increasingly private. The compulsive nature of the enterprise makes it a perfect metaphor for a world without a clearly defined beginning or ending. The gambler can get in or out at will, creating the most arbitrary termini, as Lydgate discovers when, in debt, he visits the Green Dragon:

> He had looked on at a great deal of gambling in Paris, watching it as if it had been a disease. He was no more tempted by such winning than he was by drink. He had said to himself that the only winning he cared for must be attained by a conscious process of high, difficult combination tending towards a benificent result. The power he longed for could not be represented by agitated fingers.
>
> But just as he had tried opium, so his thought now began to turn upon gambling—not with appetite for its excitement, but with a sort of wistful inward gaze after that easy way of getting money, which implied no asking and brought no responsibility.
>
> (chap. 66)

How the individual wins in this world has undergone a marked change. Because that which is risked is not owned at all, the gambler comes to imagine himself as triangulated, part of a "third party" dynamic in which he is merely an agent of Fate or Luck. Hence not merely the sum wagered, but the participant is de-objectified, creating a kind of self-delusion that he is not gambling at all. Gambling is a metaphor that George Eliot seems to have been fond of, for she places Gwendolen Harleth at a continental gaming table at the commencement of *Daniel Deronda*. It would seem to be part of the attempt to put an arbitrary value and often an arbitrary utility upon those objects and those people who have lost sight of Origins, whether it be Bulstrode's gambling "loan" to Lydgate upon administering Raffles's death, or Trumbull's activity at another raffle, where not merely value, but the identification of the object is a function of exchange:

> "Now, ladies," said Mr. Trumbull, taking up one of the articles, "this tray contains a very recherchy lot—a *collection* of trifles for the drawing-room table—and trifles make the sum of human things—nothing more important than trifles—(yes, Mr. Ladislaw, yes, by-and-by)—but pass the tray round, Joseph—these bijoux must be examined, ladies. This I have in my hand is an ingenious contrivance—a sort of practical rebus I may call it: here, you see, it looks like an elegant heart-shaped box, portable—for the pocket; there, again, it becomes like a splendid double flower—an ornament for the table; and now"—Mr.

> Trumbull allowed the flower to fall alarmingly into strings of heart-shaped leaves—"a book of riddles! No less than five hundred printed in beautiful red."
>
> (chap. 60, italics mine)

The amount bid may not reflect the value of the object at all, but rather serves to create it, at least for the buyer.

Part of Trumbull's pitch consists of an attempt to convince his audience that a particular *objet d'art* inherits some secret of the old masters now lost forever—another way of saying that it is a fragment—or to otherwise lend history to the piece by positing a fictional past that will be revealed in the future:

> Suppose it should be discovered hereafter that a gem of art has been amongst us in this town, and nobody in Middlemarch awake to it.
>
> (chap. 60)

In urging Middlemarchers to bet on it, Trumbull is doing much the same as George Eliot's narrator did with regard to Lydgate: "He was at a starting-point which makes many a man's career a fine subject for betting" (chap. 15). The one upon whom we gamble tends to become a gambler in George Eliot when the starting-point is threatened or doubted. His career or the career of the object becomes vulnerable to numerous translations upon the recognition of discontinuity. A "text" of riddles that is itself a riddle is a sure emblem of that condition of sourcelessness.

The linguistic condition corresponding to the fluidity of enterprise would be gossip, that attempt by diverse mouths to approach an original truth which seems to recede into the distance. Although Casaubon had early in *Middlemarch* cautioned Dorothea against the "mirage of baseless opinion" (chap. 20) as an excuse for prolonged research, the course of the novel makes abundantly clear that floating opinions—gossip—has a determining power that is remarkably efficient:

> News is often dispersed as thoughtlessly and effectively as that pollen which the bees carry off (having no idea how powdery they are) when they are buzzing in search of their particular nectar.
>
> (chap. 59)

In *Middlemarch* gossip always precedes the revelation of facts and is often a reasonable facsimile to such an extent that it has the appearance of determining the facts. It is commentary and conjecture most often disguising itself as an account of Origins:

> The statement was passed on until it had quite lost the stamp
> of inference, and was taken as information coming straight
> from Garth, so that even a diligent historian might have con-
> cluded Caleb to be the chief publisher of Bulstrode's
> misdemeanors.
>
> (chap. 71)

It is surely part of that "power of generalising which gives men so much
the superiority in mistake over the dumb animals" (chap. 58). The last
quarter of the novel is almost entirely spent in unravelling the relationship
between gossip and the scandal that envelopes first Bulstrode and then
Lydgate as a consequence of Raffles's mysterious death. It is not the presence of an Origin, but its very opposite, the absence of material Origin,
that promotes the linguistic "filler" that is gossip: "In this case there was
no material object to feed upon, but the eye of reason saw a probability of
mental sustenance in the shape of gossip" (chap. 71).

In this sense gossip represents a fundamental departure from a consciousness fascinated with historical tributaries or within the confines of
the pigeonholes; gossip is a notoriously elastic meta-language which con-
fuses creation and translation, in the process arbitrarily locating its own
centre. Rosamond is shocked to realize that she has "married a man who
had become the centre of infamous suspicions" (chap. 75). Additionally,
gossip would seem to achieve far more than the Reform Bill in democra-
tizing the increasingly mobile population of Middlemarch. Since any individual is free to make his own additions or deletions from a "received"
story without incurring the fear of a single authorial responsibility, the
elite like Bulstrode can be levelled anonymously. In short, gossip is a mar-
vellous paradox: it is an authorless language which creates its own public
authority for the very reason that it can never be more than a fragment.
As such, its virulence serves as an oblique commentary upon the work of
all the *originators* in *Middlemarch,* for the very form of the mode is tanta-
mount to an acknowledgment of its status as a corrupted text:

> Everybody liked better to conjecture how the thing was, than
> to know it; for conjecture soon became more confident than
> knowledge, and had a more liberal allowance for the
> incompatible.
>
> (chap. 71)

Gossip can never have an archaeology, because it is an ever-growing consciousness, obsessively displacing absence. It has a life of its own, devoid
of determinable beginning or ending. This language which assumes the

status of a mass epic in *Middlemarch* is centreless in such a way that it resembles, not just a little, the Raffles who so suddenly appears out of the
past. When asked to go to his home, the ill man replies that he cannot
because he has no fixed location to call home. Like Raffles and the gam-
blers, the life of the gossip is the life of rootless "speculation," and hence
without ending.

The transformation of a world permeated by what Comte called "the
vain quest after absolutes" into the antecedentless realm of systemic adaptation, the collapse of linear succession into the tangled skein of "circumstance," the expanded middle, leaves an impact upon consciousness and
community. There arises the confrontation of a plurality of selves, more
or less discontinuous, with a field of problems to be dealt with on an *ad
hoc* basis. Perhaps this helps to account for the shift in narrative dimension
within George Eliot's novel. The first four books, so characterized by the
epical convention of high relief, give way to the flattened plane that so
many critics have noted—that shallowing of the third dimension, background, which transforms a frieze into a tapestry or a spider web. This
marks a displacement, really, from the spaces shaped by a conviction in
some uniqueness which is imagined to lie behind any *progressus* into a belief that any problem is one of translation, interpretation, or adaptation.
And this latter activity involves the fluidity of fitting and trimming rather
than the single-mindedness of questing or terminating. Perhaps Farebrother's comments are the most apropos, since his metaphor combines
the shallowed possibilities of determination from any fixed point, but
compensates by posing the possibility of some triumph of the therapeutic.
Redemption suddenly does not require an Origin:

> "But, my dear Mrs. Casaubon," said Mr. Farebrother, smil-
> ing greatly at her ardour, "character is not cut in marble—it is
> not something solid and unalterable. It is something living and
> changing and may become diseased as our bodies do."
>
> (chap. 72)

This flatness gives an increasingly neutral aspect to character as well
as moral prospect (vision). Rosamond Vincy behaves with a chill neutral-
ity toward Lydgate, a phrase repeated several times. And when Will Ladislaw comes to collect his portfolio, for Dorothea "it was as if a crowd of
indifferent objects had thrust them asunder." Everyday details produce the
ennui that becomes part of the pathos of *Middlemarch;* the deeply etched
channels that formerly led to some reservoir of truth or knowledge have
been altered for Dorothea

in the long valley of her life, which looked so flat and empty
of way-marks, guidance would come as she walked along the
road, and saw her fellow-passengers by the way.

(chap. 77)

When life is no longer a natural sequence of events or an understood succession of descent, but rather an interpreted series, objects as well as people experience not only spatial and temporal discontinuity—the restlessness
of all the commuters in the novel—but an internal schism. Lydgate perceives not one, but two selves, "that he was getting unlike his former self"
(chap. 70) at the same time that Bulstrode recognizes that a recovered Raffles would mean the re-existence of an old Bulstrode which he cannot face.
The revelation of Ladislaw's "true" origin leads Mr. Hawley to endow
him with the physiology of a grafted hybrid, hopelessly divided:

A high-spirited young lady and a musical Polish patriot made
a likely enough stock for him to spring from, but I should
never have suspected a grafting of a Jew Pawnbroker. However, there is *no knowing what a mixture will turn out beforehand.*

(chap. 71, italics mine)

This structural mirroring is George Eliot's way of suggesting that the
deflection from one's given Origin produces a kind of schizoid split in personality. Early in the novel Casaubon had refused to acknowledge discontinuity, the likeness-in-difference that had separated his profile from that
of Aquinas. Dorothea had similarly initially identified Will Ladislaw as a
descendant from the source, the miniature that graced the walls at Lowick.
Only later when, fearing that she may never see Will again, she offers to
return the picture of his ancestor—only then, upon his refusal, is the historical internalized:

"No; I don't mind about it. It is not very consoling to have
one's own likeness. It would be more consoling if others
wanted to have it."

"I thought you would like to cherish her memory—I
thought—" Dorothea broke off in an instant, her imagination
suddenly warning her away from Aunt Julia's history—"you
would surely like to have the miniature as a family memorial."

"Why should I have that, when I have nothing else! A man
with only a portmanteau for his stowage must keep his memo-
rials in his head."

(chap. 54)

The "two-penny mirror's" reflection of some higher truth represents a misunderstanding of human existence. Dorothea must come to accept Will for what he is rather than seek to memorialize his Origin. Discontinuity is real for Will, breachable to Dorothea. Whereas she sees historical lineage, he sees only the pictorial reflection symbolizing a discontinuity that makes him an *isolato*. The emblematic episode which illustrates the necessity to acknowledge the fragmentation at the core of things occurs on the hustings during Brooke's abortive campaign. When he confronts his own echo (in the form of an effigy hung by the opposition camp) alternately expanding and contracting his speech, much in the manner of gossip, he loses the sense of a unique self and with it, the politician's motivation.

Hence, the latter two books of *Middlemarch* present the reader with a changed moral universe, partially in consequence of this alteration in the status of the Origin. For it is not merely that Lydgate's culpability remains forever indeterminate, but that even Bulstrode's role in Raffles's death is the role of the circuitous, unwilling criminal who transgresses through surrogates. His crime is one of omission rather than commission, since he simply fails to give all the details of the treatment to the attending housekeeper. Evidence is no longer to be taken as an accumulation of signs which lead to some act in the past, as it had been for Casaubon's reading of mythic traces, but rather that the evidence may well be an absence. The disappearance of the logocentric universe means, to pun upon the increasing entanglements of "circumstances," that blame is largely *circumstantial*. It represents a shift from a world illuminated by the *a priori* to a world where the determinations and judgments are always part of the greying of the *de facto*, "a pale shade of bribery which is sometimes called prosperity" (chap. 76). In one sense such a realm is one of infinite potential: it is "possible that Bulstrode was innocent of criminal intention"; "possible that he had nothing to do with [the housekeeper's] disobedience" (chap. 76); possible that Bulstrode's *de facto* cheque was not intended as a bribe. Potentiality seems to expand in direct ratio to the diminishment of externally identifiable responsibility—for anything. Casaubon had felt entirely responsible for his ward, Will Ladislaw; his is the responsibility of a relationship "not thereby annulled in [its] character of determining antecedents" (chap. 37), even after Will has visited Dorothea in his own absence. But, by the end of *Middlemarch,* beyond the crisis of the determining antecedent, direct responsibility or motive is difficult to locate and identify. And one index of this disappearance of individual motive, causality, and responsibility is the proliferation of agents, people whose sole function is that of filling the void between discontinuous groups, thereby softening authority. These folk, like the housekeeper who tends Raffles in his last illness or Bulstrode's patient wife who is enlisted (as a surrogate for Bulstrode) to give her nephew the laundered money that is his by right, exist, like the Dorothea on errand to Rosamond Vincy, as go-betweens. They create the possibility of deniability in those whom they represent, part of the transactional, therapeutic activity that deflects intentionality from a single identifiable source.

All of this may be merely an extension of that shift by which private responsibility became enlarged and flattened during the Victorian period, becoming part of the infamous General Will, the abstraction of presumed consensus. By the novel's end, the great plans for the hospital which was to be financed by private subscription are being assumed by the municipal authority and now include a projected cemetery, a preparation for contingencies (endings) rather than the research into beginnings to which Lydgate had early pledged himself. And the diseases of the last chapters—the threat of cholera from Danzig or the gout in whose attendance Lydgate culminates his sad career—are illnesses whose origins are vague by virtue of being either exotic or unknown. One is an illness of the very poor, the other, of the very rich. And Will Ladislaw, who had previously renounced any interest in the "sources of the Nile," becomes intrigued, as a penultimate scheme prior to standing for Parliament, in colonization, a tacit admission of public involvement in discontinuity—the "likeness-in-difference" of the would-be colonial administrator. It is an ironic comment upon Dorothea's realization that reform is made difficult when "everything seems like going on a mission to people whose language I don't know" (chap. 3). The notion of some essential or at least historically primary language like Hebrew or Greek, gives way progressively in *Middlemarch* to a proliferation of discontinuous, often unique, languages that must be understood on their own terms: gossip; the interchangeable adjectives of the auctioneer; the redundantly legalistic language of wills; the babbling rhetoric of poor Brooke on the campaign trail; Hawley's "awful language"; and finally, the metonymic language of the child or the childish. None are corrupt because none are pure.

George Eliot's novel itself participates in the same displacement from Origins which her characters undergo. In the supplementary chapter beyond the ending, appropriately entitled finale, her narrator assents to entirely arbitrary distinctions between the limits that originate and those that terminate: "Every limit is a beginning as well as an ending" (finale). In so recognizing the network of conditional relationships as opposed to the narrow lineage of historically ordered descent, she echoes the effusive Mrs. Cadwallader who, in explaining the woes of the clergyman's wife, listened to her husband's sermons backwards—first the ending, then the middle, and finally, the beginning, because she "couldn't have the end without them" (chap. 34). Origins are only pragmatic, as Will Ladislaw realizes early on. In his debate with Lydgate, the doctor had insisted that Ladislaw's writings for the *Pioneer* constituted a betrayal, because they had led people to believe that society can be healed by the political process. Ladislaw's "text," as he calls it, has as its objective only the balancing of claims:

> That's very fine, my dear fellow. But your cure must begin somewhere, and put it that a thousand things which debase a population can never be reformed without this particular reform to begin with.
>
> (chap. 46)

Ladislaw is here distinguishing, like George Eliot in the opening sentence of the finale, between an Origin and a beginning, between some whole sacred source, and an arbitrary limit whose function is only denotative.

The growing good of the world comes to be dependent not upon those determining antecedents, which turn out to be functional rather than real, but on "unhistoric acts" and "unvisited tombs." The attempt to define Lydgate's "fair unknown," the "primitive tissue," is transformed into an extention of the therapeutic, the business of obligatory servicing. Fred Vincy produces a sort of Victorian do-it-yourself book on the *Cultivation of Green Crops and the Economy of Cattle-Feeding* while his wife *translates* and *adapts* one of the ancients, Plutarch, into a "little book for boys," not exactly Casaubon's *magnum opus,* but a document of sorts. And the quest for some single, uncorrupted author(ity) at the heart of the matter seems superfluous to Middlemarchers who cannot decide whether the author is Fred or Mary:

> In this way it was made clear that Middlemarch had never been deceived, and there was no need to praise anybody for writing a book, since it was always done by somebody else.
>
> (finale)

Motivation, responsibility for good or evil, is relativized by the absence at the Origin, and that absence creates, in place of the attempt to clarify that which came before, a systemically ordered mode of exchange. Will and Dorothea are "bound to each other by a love stronger than any impulses which could have marred it" and Will is returned to Parliament by a "constituency who paid his expenses" (finale), suggesting that the business of life involves emotional and political balancing acts rather than reform—an emphasis upon the "bottom line" mentality of the business statement rather than the martyred quest for some antecedent unity. The conclusion of the novel is filled with images of people in motion: Will commutes from London; the two sisters visit one another's children with increasing frequency; and the community scurries about its business. All, by the end of the novel, are commuters, participants in a decentred universe, where, as George Eliot would have it in her prelude, people are "*dispersed* among hindrances, instead of *centering* in some long-recognizable deed." It is a world no longer characterized by pigeonholes of containment or "plans" for cottages, but rather by socially regulated locomotion.

In George Eliot's finale, which matches other conclusions in Middlemarch in its arbitrary, flat, guide-book tone, gambling has been institutionalized in Lydgate's heavy life insurance policy which, somewhat fortuitously, "makes" Rosamond. Gossip no longer indicts or motivates, but indulges itself in the leisure of *de facto* negative prescriptions: "she ought not to have married Will Ladislaw" (finale). The passive voice dominates our Endings, detached as they are from the grounding of a definable sacred. For the point, made best by Farebrother, is that the sacred is whatever we will it to be: "he had just set up a pair of beautiful goats to be pets of the village *in general*, and to walk at large as sacred animals" (chap. 80, italics mine). Whether it be umbrella rings or goats for children, objects have a potentiality no longer determined by antecedents. The evidence suggests that the sacred is not to be defined by a process analogous to self-consciousness in its devotion to recovery, but rather that its outlet is transitive. One of the most symbolic scenes in the novel occurs when Celia refuses to mourn the deceased Casaubon, directing her thoughts toward a different "orientalist," her child.

> "We should not grieve, should we, baby?" said Celia confidentially to that unconscious centre and poise of the world, who had the most remarkable fists all complete even to his nails, and hair enough, really when you took his cap off, to make—you didn't know what:—in short, he was Bouddha in a Western form.
>
> (chap. 50)

In a world where Casaubon's "remote source of knowledge," Lydgate's "primary tissue," and Bulstrode's "sacred accountability," to borrow their respective nomenclature of Origins, no longer have primacy, the centre is not self-consciousness, but the unconscious and the unhistoric—the child. And the children who emerge as the foci of their parents' communities in the twilight of *Middlemarch,* like George Eliot's own narrative finale itself, create their own arbitrarily fictional, indeterminate Endings—the coda to our Origin-bound, egoistic epics.

Knowledge in *Middlemarch*

Alexander Welsh

Most of the principal characters in *Middlemarch* have as their aim, in one form or another, the pursuit of knowledge. Edward Casaubon and Tertius Lydgate are the two most obviously dedicated, and determined to make a name for themselves, in this pursuit. Each envisions his research as systematic, over a unified field: hence Casaubon is preparing his famous Key to all Mythologies, and Lydgate believes that a "fundamental knowledge of structure" (chap. 15) is important to medical practice. Neither finds his task smooth going, and Casaubon finds it particularly rough going against the narrator's very evident skepticism and scathing commentary. "Such capacity of thought and feeling as had ever been stimulated in him by the general life of mankind had long shrunk to a sort of dried preparation, a lifeless embalmment of knowledge" (chap. 20), for example—and even the "such" is sharply qualifying. In the course of the novel George Eliot impugns Casaubon's scholarship (chap. 21) and finally dismisses the Key as something a good deal less than scientific "error," which sometimes leads to truth. "Mr. Casaubon's theory . . . was not likely to bruise itself unawares against discoveries"; it is "not tested," not falsifiable, in fact, and therefore not science (chap. 48). The novelist sympathizes with Casaubon and is close to him in some ways—both she and Lewes associated the character with themselves—but clearly she is much more respectful of Lydgate's pursuit of knowledge. The latter's "clearest eye for probabilities" and "fullest obedience to knowledge" are to his credit, despite his shallow regard for women's knowledge and other blindnesses. He has, at least in

From *George Eliot and Blackmail*. © 1985 by the President and Fellows of Harvard College. Harvard University Press, 1985.

science, a "testing vision of details and relations" and a readiness "to invent tests." And Lydgate is very modern in his stated preference for information over something called justice: "People talk about evidence," he remarks, "as if it could really be weighed in scales by blind Justice. No man can judge what is good evidence on any particular subject, unless he knows that subject well" (chap. 16). His pride, of course, is exposed in nearly all such accounts of his mind, and he will come to realize that he can be trapped by circumstances notwithstanding his knowledge and essential probity. Though George Eliot is kinder to him than she is to Casaubon, Lydgate's pursuit of knowledge also entails forms of blindness.

But why always Casaubon and Lydgate? Just because knowledge is a deep subject, let us not forget Mr. Brooke. As [Gillian] Beer has observed, "One should always pay attention to Mr. Brooke." With his "documents" (chap. 2) and "love of knowledge, and going into everything" (chap. 5), he is like a caricature of Casaubon and Lydgate. "Those germinal ideas of making his mind tell upon the world at large which had been present in him from his younger years, but had hitherto lain in some obstruction, had been sprouting under cover," with the result that Mr. Brooke has purchased the *Pioneer* and is bent upon influencing public opinion (chap. 37). He is, in truth, the single character in the novel most closely associated with public opinion, which in its positive aspect has become almost a joke, presented in Dickensian high spirits: "and what do we meet for but to speak our minds—freedom of opinion, freedom of the press, liberty—that kind of thing?" (chap. 51). It is astonishing how quickly George Eliot has moved from a celebration of public opinion in the abstract in *Felix Holt* to this lighter treatment; and a corresponding adjustment has occurred in regard to the Reform Bill. It is the same bill and the same period in both novels, but viewed seemingly from greater distance now. Mr. Brooke may be a fool, but there is a greater tolerance for fools and for reform in *Middlemarch*. He is a person with good intentions and "plenty of ideas and facts," who merely needs Will Ladislaw "to put them into shape" (chap. 34). [U.C.] Knoepflmacher has suggested that Mr. Brooke has a representative nineteenth-century mind, and before he is dismissed as merely silly, or his silliness deemed unworthy, it ought to be remembered that he bears some family resemblance to Dorothea Brooke, who also longs to accomplish some good, and who imagined she would find purpose in "the fellowship in high knowledge" (chap. 48). Similarly, Camden Farebrother, one of the least blameworthy characters in *Middlemarch*, is more interested in natural history and in the scientific literature of the day than he is in his ministry, and is furthermore reported—somewhat scandalously for a man in his position—to favor "Brougham and Useful Knowledge" (chap. 38).

Nicholas Bulstrode also pursues knowledge, though his researches may not be directly apparent because what he deliberately seeks is error. "To point out other people's errors," we are told, "was a duty that Mr. Bulstrode rarely shrank from" (chap. 13), and there can be no doubt that he has acquired valuable information in fulfilling this duty. If the powerlessness of Mr. Brooke's knowledge is self-evident, and his influence upon public opinion something of a joke, the power of Bulstrode is real. Indeed, in Middlemarch only Bulstrode is in a position to realize the adage that knowledge is power, and his power takes a peculiarly unpleasant cast:

> Mr. Bulstrode's power was not due simply to his being a country banker, who knew the financial secrets of most traders in the town and could touch the springs of their credit; it was fortified by a beneficence that was at once ready and severe . . . He would take a great deal of pains about apprenticing Tegg the shoemaker's son, and he would watch over Tegg's churchgoing; he would defend Mrs. Strype the washerwoman against Stubb's unjust exaction on the score of her drying-ground, and he would himself scrutinize a calumny against Mrs. Strype. His private minor loans were numerous, but he would inquire strictly into the circumstances both before and after. In this way a man gathers a domain in his neighbours' hope and fear as well as gratitude; and power, when once it has got into that subtle region, propagates itself spreading out of all proportion to its external means. It was a principle with Mr. Bulstrode to gain as much power as possible, that he might use it for the glory of God.
>
> (chap. 16)

Thus Bulstrode knows, watches, scrutinizes, and inquires his way to power. The last sentence is the clue to the systematic claim of his project. His belief in Providence is as firm as Casaubon's in the common origin of myths or Lydgate's in the common structure of living tissue, and a lot steadier than Brooke's faith in the march of mind. He believes he has access to that body of knowledge which is divine Providence, as later chapters of the novel make clear. "He was doctrinally convinced that there was a total absence of merit in himself; but that doctrinal conviction may be held . . . with intense satisfaction when the depth of our sinning is but a measure for the depth of forgiveness, and a clenching proof that we are peculiar instruments of the divine intention" (chap. 53). Bulstrode, too, is a man of ratiocination and proofs, and he is a man of truth, a man who "shrank from a direct lie with an intensity disproportionate to the number of his more indirect misdeeds" (chap. 68).

Any such partial catalogue of the characters of *Middlemarch* argues that this study of provincial life, first, invents a good many quests for knowledge and, second, calls every one of the quests in doubt. The epic theme, moreover, is confirmed by the hero and heroine who stand against knowledge in the abstract, who are the conservative and least modern of all the characters, and who enjoy the nearly unqualified admiration of the novelist, a writer of no little erudition herself. I refer, of course, to Caleb Garth and his daughter Mary, whose main action is to keep well clear of the other heroes and heroines and to rescue from the incongruous effects of a classical education one Fred Vincy, in order to perpetuate their conservative race. Caleb Garth is George Eliot's hero of work, of getting things done. He can think and calculate, but his head is never divorced from his hand, and his knowledge is therein equivalent to skill. He is notably not one to keep a close accounting of what others owe him. He works for work's sake and not because he is driven by the market. He loves to contemplate the "myriad-headed, myriad-handed labour by which the social body is fed, clothed, and housed," but this is his practical and organic idea of community, not a systematic idea of society. "His classification of human employments was rather crude, and . . . would not be acceptable in these advanced times." Only "business," defined as practical work, interests him, and "learning" is pointedly one of the activities his classification leaves to one side:

> He divided [employments] into "business, politics, preaching, learning, and amusement." He had nothing to say against the last four; but he regarded them as a reverential pagan regarded other gods than his own. In the same way he thought very well of all ranks, but he would not himself have liked to be of any rank in which he had not such close contact with "business" as to get often honourably decorated with marks of dust and mortar, the damp of the engine, or the sweet soil of the woods and fields.
>
> (chap. 24)

The daughter of this man of business is Mary Garth, a young woman of great steadiness and loyalty who considers her father and mother "the best part of myself" (chap. 25) and who would rather be at home than go off to be a teacher (chap. 40). She utterly rejects "preaching" as an employment for Fred Vincy and patiently waits until he can be helped into "business" by her father. When they marry, Fred will have forgotten his Greek and Latin (chap. 86), and in the finale of the novel we read that Mary gives her own children—who are boys, unlike Rosamond Lydgate's girls—"little formal teaching."

Middlemarch is not only concerned with the limitations of knowledge but with the close bearing of motives of reputation on knowledge. In *Felix Holt* the juxtaposition of a positive public opinion and crude blackmail expresses this relation; in *Middlemarch* the relation of knowing to being known is persistently and finely drawn in each of the stories, so that the extreme case of blackmailing Bulstrode is but one of four relevant actions. Casaubon, Lydgate, Brooke, and Bulstrode are every one susceptible to threatening publicity. It is as if George Eliot were saying that the pursuit of knowledge, in modern society, is not separable from questions of publicity. If knowledge itself is remote, storable in "documents," exchangeable, publishable, and sometimes concealable, then the same effects of distance that govern its being govern also its practitioners, who are thereby subject to exposure in a way very different from Caleb Garth's experience. Garth is known personally for the work he does and can do; the seekers of knowledge have placed themselves at risk in a culture of information, a culture that can inform against them.

George Eliot makes abundantly clear that virtually the sole motive of Casaubon's scholarship is fame, and that this relation between his knowledge and his being known runs far deeper than mere vanity, his pleasure in sitting for the portrait of St. Thomas Aquinas and the like. Casaubon is both vain and "resolute in being a man of honour," a person "unimpeachable by any recognized opinion"; but he is subject to the deepest terror by authorship. He will be judged in absentia from his writings, and already is so judged, as he fears. Authorship entails risks that are less within his control than his personal conduct.

> In conduct these ends [of honor] had been attained; but the difficulty of making his Key to all Mythologies unimpeachable weighed like lead upon his mind; and the pamphlets—or "Parerga," as he called them—by which he tested his public and deposited small monumental records of his march, were far from having been seen in all their significance. He suspected the Archdeacon of not having read them; he was in painful doubt as to what was really thought of them by the leading minds of Brasenose, and bitterly convinced that his old acquaintance

> Carp had been the writer of that depreciatory recension which
> was kept locked in a small drawer of Mr. Casaubon's desk, and
> also in a dark closet of his verbal memory. These were heavy
> impressions to struggle against, and brought that melancholy
> embitterment which is the consequence of all excessive claim:
> even his religious faith wavered with his wavering trust in his
> own authorship, and the consolations of the Christian hope in
> immortality seemed to lean on the immortality of the still un-
> written Key to all Mythologies.

The independent life of writing, divorced from its author, becomes a
strong reason for not writing at all, lest some terrible failure in the Key—
like a previous mistake in a dedication of a Parergon to Carp—open the
author "to ridicule in the next age" or to "be chuckled over by Pike and
Trench in the present" (chap. 29). George Eliot knew of the terror herself,
as the recension put away in the locked drawer may suggest by resemblance to the drawer to which Lewes consigned even those writings about
the novelist that he approved. Scholarship has its good days, and Dr.
Spanning's praise of "my late tractate on the Egyptian Mysteries" puts Casaubon in a rare good humor (chap. 37), but on the whole the perils out-
weigh the pleasures. When Will Ladislaw, "not at all deep himself in German writers," criticizes Casaubon's failure to consult the Germans who
"have taken the lead in historical inquiries," the narrator comments wryly
that "mortals are easily tempted to pinch the life out of their neighbour's
buzzing glory, and think that such killing is no murder" (chap. 21). The
equation of this diminishment of reputation with murder, however light-
heartedly represented as insecticide, connects with the one murder case in
Middlemarch, which is in response to blackmail, and may recall that at the
beginning of this century blackmail was popularly referred to as "moral
murder."

The importance of Lydgate's relation to his public is more evident because he is a doctor. In the nature of such a career, he must not only know
what he is doing but be perceived as knowing. His success is bound to
depend on public relations that ostensibly have little to do with medical
science. Lydgate's particular failure, therefore, follows from his neglect
and scorn for this aspect of the practitioner's life, just as his ironic success
in later years depends more on being fashionable than on scientific achievement. But Lydgate is more than just a doctor, and is far closer than Casaubon to George Eliot's idea of an intellectual. His troubles both personal
and professional conflict with an ideal. "Only those who know the su-
premacy of the intellectual life—the life which has a seed of ennobling

thought and purpose within it—can understand the grief of one who falls from that serene activity into the absorbing soul-wasting struggle with worldly annoyances" (chap. 73). Some of Lydgate's troubles result from his finely described "commonness," or unconscious snobbery—a taking for granted of status that fatally ignores opinion. He does begin to understand, what had not occurred to him, that even popularity may interfere with a career, as when his talent attracts Rosamond "because it gives him prestige, and is like an order in his button-hole or an Honourable before his name" (chap. 58). Lydgate's is the most sharply differentiated talent in *Middlemarch*: in his intellectual aim and in his specialization he is the most modern hero of the novel, and the constraint that his marriage places upon him is partly due to what Georg Simmel analyzed as the typically differentiated relations of modern men, which prompt concealment in several directions at once.

> These differentiated friendships which connect us with one individual in terms of affection, with another, in terms of common intellectual aspects, with a third, in terms of religious impulses, and with a fourth, in terms of common experiences— all these friendships present a very peculiar synthesis in regard to the question of discretion, of reciprocal revelation and concealment. They require that the friends do not look into those mutual spheres of interest and feeling which, after all, are not included in the relation and which, if touched upon, would make them feel painfully the limits of their mutual understanding.
>
> [*The Sociology of George Simmel*, trans. and ed. by Kurt H. Wolff]

The analysis is extremely suggestive of Lydgate's partial relations with his fellow doctors, with Bulstrode, with Farebrother, with Ladislaw, with his family, and with his own wife, no one of which relations admits of frank intimacy. Without question Rosamond's concealments from her husband are stunning, but as perceptive students of that marriage have begun to comment, he is not open with her. Nor can Lydgate, the most promising and undoubtedly talented seeker of knowledge, be open with any of the Middlemarchers: it is this isolation that makes Dorothea's befriending of him so touching. George Eliot hints at some tragic flaw in the "commonness" of Lydgate (chap. 15), but succeeds brilliantly in portraying the common relations of a modern person with his fellows. This intellectual's embroilment with Bulstrode and his recognition that even "valid evidence" will not clear him (chap. 73) dramatize his position beyond a doubt. It is the nature of his position in society that it will not support him by close friendships, and it is the nature of opinion and circumstances to indict.

George Eliot studies the connection between the pursuit of knowledge and the opinion of others with a reserved pathos in the case of Casaubon and with marvelous subtlety in the case of Lydgate. For Mr. Brooke she deploys some light comic reversals that can be enjoyed by all. It is only right that a fool who longs to exercise his love of knowledge "and that kind of thing" in the public arena should learn at first hand how he is regarded by the public. Hence Brooke as publisher of the *Pioneer* meets with an unflattering description of himself in the *Trumpet* (chap. 38), and is told to his face by his tenant Dagley that his "charrickter" in Middlemarch is nothing to be proud of (chap. 39). For Bulstrode, also, there is a sharp reversal in store, in which poetic justice takes a somewhat melodramatic turn. Since Bulstrode's power flows from his knowledge of the errors or weaknesses of others, it is only right that he should fall victim to Raffles's blackmail and inadvertent revelation of his secret. The novelist sets up Bulstrode for a fall just as surely as she sets up Brooke, but the fall is to be singular and complete—not the fall of a great criminal, as in an old form of tragedy, but of a man of high pretensions. "For the pain, as well as the public estimate of disgrace, depends on the amount of previous profession. To men who only aim at escaping felony, nothing short of the prisoner's dock is disgrace. But Bulstrode had aimed at being an eminent Christian" (chap. 53). If the demonstration in some respects is rather crude, in other respects, such as the relation of Bulstrode to his wife, it is very fine. Moreover, the applications of this fall are to be taken to heart by all. "Who can know how much of his most inward life is made up of the thoughts he believes other men to have about him, until that fabric of opinion is threatened with ruin?" (chap. 68).

The rare characters in *Middlemarch* who are immune to opinion and uninterested in scandal are the very same—the Garths—who stand against knowledge in the abstract. Caleb Garth is present when Raffles first accosts Bulstrode, but he immediately takes himself off: "if there was anything discreditable to be found out concerning another man, Caleb prefered not to know it" (chap. 53). Nevertheless—and this is one of the final ironies of the novel—Garth is instrumental in bringing about Bulstrode's fall. He cannot abide a life that is double: therefore, as soon as he has heard the story, he ceases to work for one who "can't get his life clear" (chap. 69). Though Garth says nothing to anyone, his ending of his employment is taken in Middlemarch to be a direct criticism of the banker, "so that even a diligent historian might have concluded Caleb to be the chief publisher of Bulstrode's misdemeanours" (chap. 71). George Eliot deliberately calls attention to Garth's role even as she exonerates him: his is the stern judgment against which a divided life finally breaks. Without some such tribunal blackmail itself would be futile, and by making Garth seem to be, though he is not, "the chief publisher" of Bulstrode's faults, the novelist admits that Raffles operates with the best opinion positively behind him.

Garth's daughter Mary is similarly disinclined to interfere in the affairs of others. She guards against even the appearance of wrong when she nurses Featherstone on his deathbed (chap. 33); she "looks about her, but does not suppose that anybody is looking at her" (chap. 40). Dorothea Casaubon, on the other hand, is a curious exception in this regard. Her actions are not dictated by "the world's opinion" either (chap. 48), and she believes "that people are almost always better than their neighbours think they are" (chap. 72), yet unlike Mary or Caleb Garth she is one of the seekers after knowledge in the novel.

A formidable case for Dorothea has been made by the very students of George Eliot who have made of *Middlemarch* a book of knowledge—or a book of wisdom. By carefully tracing the ways in which Lydgate and Dorothea are complementary characters, U.C. Knoepflmacher shows how the Arnoldian balance of virtues tips in her favor: "Lydgate's gradual fall and Dorothea's gradual ascendancy" argue that she gains, in the course of the novel, "the true disinterestedness that was lacking in his . . . idealism." After reviewing the role of hypothesis, of imagination, and of active feeling that Lewes, especially, stressed in scientific work, George Levine has taken the comparison with Lydgate one step further and suggested that Dorothea is ironically "the better scientist." And David Carroll has analyzed the way in which "the ideas of perception, hypothesis, and evidence" enter into the series of actions near the end in which Dorothea weighs the facts and reaches important conclusions with respect to Lydgate and Ladislaw. For in "the climax" of the novel it is up to Dorothea to make a clear judgment of "the circumstantial evidence" seeming to link Lydgate financially with Bulstrode and Ladislaw sexually with Rosamond. Carroll shows how the heroine, in remaining flexible and forcing herself to be disengaged, can arrive at the true facts much as a scientist ought to. "The mind must move flexibly and disinterestedly among the circumstances, untrammelled by deduction. . . . Instead of excluding the circumstances which threaten her beliefs, she must absorb them into a more comprehensive hypothesis." In other words, when Dorothea returns to the foreground of the action in *Middlemarch*, she copes successfully by employing scientific methods that have little resemblance to the "high knowledge" that she dreamed of at the beginning.

If such interpretations are correct in their tendency, then one still has to wonder a little about the apparent exemption of the heroine from the desire of fame, and from the onus of reputation as well. Two explanations of Dorothea's exemption are possible. Recent defenses of her devotion to truth are so congruent with the Leweses' ideas of science, that one has to step back from them a little and recall that she is not, after all, engaged in an activity very much like scientific research. Dorothea is trying to understand what is happening among the people she knows and forcing herself, in the case she cares most about, to extend the benefit of doubt. Neither in her marriage choices nor in other personal relations does she concern herself with public opinion. Carroll makes a special point of her "act of belief" in Lydgate, and so does George Eliot (the expression is Lydgate's own, in direct discourse). In truth, the heroine's direct, personal response to Lydgate ignores both public opinion and the evidence. Carroll's use of the word "nobility" suggests the archaic quality of her response, and in effect the relations of society are abridged by this heroic performance.

The other possibility is that Doreathea is no exception at all to the other characters' interest in fame, once her performance has been publicized by the writing of *Middlemarch*. With corrosive insight Calvin Bedient has written of the "famished need for recognition" in the novel and of fame as its theme. "The effort—and failure—of self-monumentalization embraces almost the entire cast. Nearly every important character tries to carve his name on the world—to become as permanent as history, as significant as all mankind." Bedient's hyperbole has the ring of outrageous truth, and if Dorothea's personality is unlike the rest of the cast's, her presentation in the Prelude and Finale of the novel tells another story. The argument of the former is that modern girls cannot look forward to the fame of Saint Theresa, and of the latter, that it is a shame they will rest in unvisited tombs. Within the novel proper the superiority of the heroine exerts itself so as to make her lack of fame all the more regrettable. In this inverted interpretation of *Middlemarch* Dorothea remains central, and Bedient has glimpsed her helplessness before the culture of information.

In the present interpretation of the novel I am conscious of fighting shy of Dorothea, as we know—from the maintenance of a multiple plot, the study of the other side of her marriage, and the expenditure of humor at her expense—that the novelist herself fought shy of the heroine, without entirely succeeding. Dorothea is significantly less modern than any of the other seekers of knowledge—Casaubon, Lydgate, Brooke, Bulstrode, and even Farebrother. Her plight as a woman is hardly specific to the nineteenth century, as the example of Romola partially attests. If George Eliot had wished, she might have given her heroine a career, but convention and inclination were against it. She may project the "common yearning of womanhood" (the language of the prelude is obscure) in Dorothea more than in any other character, but the novels given much to projection—*Romola* and to a lesser extent *The Mill on the Floss*—are now well behind her. In Dorothea's two marriages there is not a marked question of discontinuity, as we might expect, but rather a kind of persistent virginity in the face of both. I am less struck, finally, by the degree to which Dorothea changes in the course of the novel than the degree to which, like many heroines, she remains a given. In almost the first sentence of *Middlemarch* we read that this heroine has "the impressiveness of a fine quotation from the Bible—or from one of our elder poets—in a paragraph of today's newspaper" (chap. 1). That comparison, to say nothing of the one with Italian paintings of the Virgin, immediately registers the archaism of the character and opposes her to the print culture of the nineteenth century.

Two other of the seekers of knowledge are also rather static, and the manner in which they are presented is essentially sportive, comic as well as partial. Casaubon and Brooke are alike in the futility and the internal disconnectedness of their enterprises—the clutter of notations awaiting pigeonholes. Brooke is the more nearly static of the two, but Casaubon is not much better: all he ultimately learns is that marriage to a young woman is extremely uncomfortable for him. There is a strong element of the comic in the conception of Brooke and Casaubon both, less of the comic in Dorothea and Farebrother, but a sense in which all three male characters, at least, stay pretty much in place. They belong in the neighborhood, and their lives are not threatened by discontinuity in the sense that we have been remarking. Lydgate and Bulstrode, on the other hand, do not belong to Middlemarch, do not live continuous lives, do have careers that matter, and are profoundly changed in the end. The lives of Lydgate and Bulstrode tend least to comic resolution, and they are, especially as they appear in combination, the most modern of the characters concerned with knowledge. The two, indeed, are closely tied together in the narrative, and I hope to move closer to the significance of information, and of blackmail, in *Middlemarch* by thinking about their relation.

From the meeting of the board of the infirmary early in the novel to the occasion of Raffles's illness and death, with its "malignant effect on Lydgate's reputation" (chap. 71), the banker and the doctor are bound together in a special way. Significantly, they are not friends and have antithetical feelings and personalities; they are brought into conjunction by their specialized functions within a modern social organization. Lydgate "did not intend to be a vassal of Bulstrode's" (chap. 18), and the choice of word for the excluded relation is significant. It is part of Lydgate's modern consciousness that he needs only "a medium for his work" or "a vehicle for his ideas," no personal and distinctly archaic relation to another more powerful than himself; and likewise Bulstrode's power is not based on fealty in the community but on information and credit. Nonetheless it is Lydgate's connection with Bulstrode, mirrored by his alienation from his wife, that comes to symbolize the most arcane power of circumstances in the novel, and thus George Eliot's most radical representation of society.

"On this occasion," the narrator informs us, "Bulstrode became identified with Lydgate," and she presents the meeting of the infirmary board as Lydgate's first real brush with circumstances:

> For the first time Lydgate was feeling the hampering threadlike pressure of small social conditions, and their frustrating complexity. At the end of his inward debate, when he set out for the hospital, his hope was really in the chance that discussion might somehow give a new aspect to the question, and make the scale dip so as to exclude the necessity for voting. I think he trusted a little also to the energy which is begotten by circumstances,—some feeling rushing warmly and making resolve easy, while debate in cool blood had only made it more difficult.
>
> (chap. 18)

If there is a recollection of Lilliput in the first image, it merely puts a satiric edge to the description of individual and social perplexity. The following image, of the balance scale, brings together Lydgate's science with the operation of opinion, since he hopes that discussion will render voting unnecessary. The dipping of a laboratory scale, on which some scientific truth depends, is already an image that makes knowledge seem fragile; and the same implication extends to opinion at the meeting. That a scientist who has been unable to decide a question calmly by himself trusts to feelings at a meeting to decide it for him is not a slap at Lydgate alone, but a reflection on how collective decisions are arrived at. The thought anticipates, to be sure, the ironic conclusion of the scene in which Lydgate, goaded by one of the other doctors, casts the deciding vote for Bulstrode's candidate for chaplain of the infirmary, but the study of this deservedly famous scene is precisely the interaction of relative strangers at a meeting, so familiar as a modern institution. Such hospital or other committees are replications in small of the wider combinations of society, and questions of discretion and concealment, revelation and power are implicit in the information that is debated there.

A Mrs. Taft in Middlemarch, "who was always counting stitches and gathered her information in misleading fragments caught between the rows of her knitting, had got it into her head that Mr. Lydgate was a natural son of Bulstrode's, a fact which seemed to justify her suspicions of evangelical laymen" (chap. 26). But Lydgate is no more a natural son to Bulstrode than he is his vassal. The doctor and banker are thrown together even though they have no personal liking for one another, and each is aware of the mixed reputation that the other enjoys in the town. They have a good deal in common, besides their association with the infirmary, in their susceptibility to comment and in the concealment of their private selves from the public. No doubt the concealments of Bulstrode are of a guilty kind and those of Lydgate less contorted, but in each the concealment is deepened by the professional role. Both lives are divided between public and private being, and the crossing of that division is experienced like a burn. In danger of exposure Bulstrode thinks of leaving Middlemarch in order to escape the "scorching" contempt of his neighbors (chap. 68), and Lydgate habitually "shrank, as from a burn, from the utterance of any word about his private affairs" (chap. 63). The professional relation of the two begins in the carefully delineated circumstances of the meeting of the board and concludes amid circumstances that make them appear accomplices in murder, "circumstances [that] would always be stronger" than anything Lydgate might say on his own behalf (chap. 73). Both characters occupy a world in which the relation of outward to inward being can only be deduced from circumstances, and in which gossip itself pretends to reason. The seeming collusion of Bulstrode and Lydgate "was soon to be loudly spoken of in Middlemarch as a necesssary 'putting of two and two together' " (chap. 71).

When the younger man's medical opinions, too rational to be readily understood perhaps, have come into dispute in the town, "Mr. Toller remarked one day, smilingly, to Mrs. Taft, that 'Bulstrode had found a man to suit him in Lydgate; a charlatan in religion is sure to like other sorts of charlatans' " (chap. 45). Again slander points to the true connection. There are plenty of grounds for arguing, from the superior vantage point of George Eliot and the reader, that Bulstrode's religion is false and Lydgate's science true, but what the two have in common is the career that opens them to attack. Implicit in the career are a progressive investment in

knowledge on the part of the individual *and* consistent approval or acquie-
sence on the part of those who employ the career—the people who purchase medical services or bank loans. At first hearing, Lydgate's career
seems very modern and Bulstrode's tinged with outdated and discredited
religion, but as Alan Mintz has argued, "Bulstrode the banker embodies
an almost classical unity of religious conviction and economic practice."
The classical representation he has in mind is the vocation of the capitalist
sketched by Max Weber, and as such Bulstrode is nearly as modern as
Lydgate. Even if he is "the most thoroughly corrupt character in the
novel," corruption is also endemic to his situation. Bulstrode is notoriously a hypocrite, but in a sense Lydgate would have to learn hypocrisy if
he were to be a success in Middlemarch. One thinks of the statement in
Romola of "the doubleness which is the pressing temptation in every public
career."

George Eliot goes rather far in the blasting of Bulstrode, and there is
undoubtedly deep antipathy in her portrayal of the pious banker. But we
should read carefully the famous passage in which she explains that Bulstrode was not a "coarse hypocrite." Fielding, the "great historian" with
whom George Eliot compares herself earlier in the novel (chap. 15), had
singled out hypocrisy in his preface to *Joseph Andrews* as one of the sources
of "the true Ridiculous" and thus fair game for the satirist. The leading
hypocrite in *Middlemarch* is not held up for ridicule but treated as the victim of blackmail, and we are invited to consider the cause of his vulnerability as if it were our own. An untruthful personality that may be laughed
to scorn in the eighteenth century has become something of a problem in
the nineteenth century, because of the increasing division in all personality
between public and private experience. When Raffles appears on the scene
with his "By Jove, Nick, it's you!" he performs the needling that the satirist used to perform, but with a difference. That "peculiar mixture of jovi-
ality and sneering" (chap. 53) typifies the blackmailer's manner because he
finds the idea that anyone has any real privacy so very amusing. Persons
are now exposed *by* their careers, which usually evoke a pretense of private
virtues from what are in reality impersonal relations. Bulstrode, according
to George Eliot, "was simply a man whose desires had been stronger than
his theoretic beliefs, and who had gradually explained the gratification of
his desires into satisfactory agreement with those beliefs. If this be hypocrisy, it is a process which shows itself occasionally in us all, to whatever
confession we belong." And "there is no general doctrine which is not capable of eating out our morality if unchecked by the deep-seated habit of
direct fellow-feeling with individual fellow-men" (chap. 61). The diffi-

culty is that modern society, as instanced in banking and medical careers, does not permit direct human relations to become habitual.

Lydgate and Bulstrode are strangers to Middlemarch. They have come there to engage in professions, to relate functionally to the Middlemarchers and not because they are indigenous members of a community—so it is hard to see what "deep-seated habit of direct fellow-feeling" can guide them in their social role. They are men with discontinuous lives whom society, for its part, is prepared to assimilate to its purposes, at least until some question is raised. "No one in Middlemarch was likely to have such a notion of Lydgate's past" as the narrator herself supplies. "Not only young virgins of that town, but gray-bearded men also, were often in haste to conjecture how a new acquaintance might be wrought into their purposes, contented with very vague knowledge as to the way in which life had been shaping him for that instrumentality" (chap. 15). There is irony here, since George Eliot implies that Lydgate's past must affect his performance in Middlemarch, but the townspeople, regarding him as an instrumentality, overlook this. Bulstrode, a much less likable man, is "considered to have done well in uniting himself with a real Middlemarch family" (chap. 11), but some "wished to know who his father and grandfather were, observing that five-and-twenty years ago nobody had ever heard of a Bulstrode in Middlemarch" (chap. 13). Instead of the narrator's sharing her irony with the reader in this case, we have hints and premonitions of a missing past that, when revealed, will overturn completely the man's reputation and foreclose his usefulness at one stroke.

In the twentieth century, with social mobility still more common, it is hard to imagine that anyone who dealt with Bulstrode would be gravely upset to discover how he carried on three decades ago in London, or that he himself would be much threatened by the revelation. The shady activity of those days, it turns out, is itself symbolic of unfortunate discontinuities, since "the business was a pawnbroker's" (chap. 61); quite apart from the possible criminal link of trading in stolen goods, a pawnbroker profits from pledges that are never redeemed, offered by persons who are trying to hold their personal estates together and who fail. The feeling for continuity among Victorians had to be very strong for such fine stories, which are not even given in the text, to grip the imagination in this symbolic way. The feeling *was* strong because continuity was threatening to change into the absence of continuity. Whereas Lydgate's failure in Middlemarch only gradually becomes evident, the experience of Bulstrode, verging upon the gothic, is like a nightmare: "it was as if he had had a loathsome dream, and could not shake off its images with their hateful kindred of sensations,—as if on all the pleasant surroundings of his life a dangerous reptile had left his slimy traces" (chap. 68).

The reptile is Raffles, another stranger to Middlemarch, and of course it is Raffles who indirectly drags down Lydgate too, because of the medical consultation at Stone Court, the loan from Bulstrode, and the previous association of the two men. Who or what does Raffles represent? Among the carefully studied characters in the novel, many famous in their own right, or among the lightly sketched local characters, "this loud red figure" is something of an excrescence, a literary type who has seemingly wandered into the wrong company. The narrator names him, among other things, "an incorporate past" that has risen before Bulstrode (chap. 53), but that hardly assures the reader of his real being. At least two recent commentators have associated Raffles with the characteristic devices of Dickens rather than of George Eliot. Peter K. Garrett calls him "the shabby double who parodies [Bulstrode's] rationalizing doctrines and revives his repressed guilt" and underlines the nightmare quality of the relation. In one of the most searching attempts to come to terms with this portion of the novel, David Carroll also invokes Dickens and argues that Raffles and Bulstrode "have each become the other's threatening extension" and "between them . . . make up one person." Moreover, Carroll sees the violent relation of the two as "a clear means of understanding what is happening in several other important relations—those between Casaubon and Dorothea, and Lydgate and Rosamond . . . the same pattern of tampering with the evidence of reality, of bribery, of blackmail, the rapid escalation of demands on each side, plotting and counter-plotting, and finally open hostility." Carroll treats the relation as far more gothic than I would—if one is to assign a generic name to this portion of *Middlemarch*, it should be sensational rather than gothic. The sensational element is apparent in the stress on evidence and the way in which Raffles serves as a conduit for information. "Certain facts have been wilfully excluded from the scheme of things," as Carroll explains. "They come roaring back in the shape of Raffles. . . . He comes back talking compulsively and blackmailing his briber. It is almost as if the unpleasant facts have taken on a life of their own."

The course of action adopted by Bulstrode is murder, but the roles of the several characters are blurred. The chapter in which the banker, against the doctor's orders, makes brandy available to Raffles is headed by an epigraph of George Eliot's own composition: "Our deeds still travel with us from afar, / And what we have been makes us what we are." The application is obviously to Bulstrode, but no doubt also to Lydgate, and most immediately to the sick man. "Bulstrode's first object after Lydgate had left Stone Court," the chapter begins, "was to examine Raffles's pockets, which he imagined were sure to carry signs in the shape of hotel-bills of the places he had stopped in, if he had not told the truth in saying that he had come straight from Liverpool." Curious transpositions occur here: Bulstrode is the hunted victim, but he goes through the blackmailer's pockets in search of evidence; Lydgate is the doctor in charge, but his prescription for the treatment of alcoholism is so advanced, and so contrary to received opinion, that the banker can easily risk altering it. Bulstrode's being, his "what we are," is uppermost in the text, but Lydgate we care more about, and Raffles is the one who has most recently traveled "from afar"—as if to embody the transience of the other two. Bulstrode prays for his blackmailer's death, and his prayer—assisted by the brandy—is answered. "As he sat there and beheld the enemy of his peace going irrevocably into silence, he felt more at rest than he had done for many months. His conscience was soothed by the enfolding wing of secrecy, which seemed just then like an angel sent down for his relief" (chap. 70). Of the three strangers to Middlemarch in the chapter, one has been sacrificed, the second experiences some temporary relief from the information that threatens to ruin him, and the third has become still more enmeshed in circumstances that tell against him.

Raffles, the stranger so sacrificed, has scarcely more character than the eminently dispensable Tracy in Alfred Hitchcock's *Blackmail*. Next to Bulstrode or Lydgate he weighs almost nothing at all, and he must clearly count for what rather than who he is in the novel. His role in the fine story of Bulstrode is obviously essential, and he is thus important to the story of Lydgate as well. If it will help to make his presence felt, he ought to be compared with Will Ladislaw—a much more substantial character, but one whom readers have also judged too lightweight for the part. It is astonishing how often Ladislaw, the only other stranger of note, is perceived by other characters as threatening, and precisely because he bears information of some kind. When he appears in Middlemarch as editor of the *Pioneer*, Mr. Hawley claims to recognize the foreign type—"some emisssary," as he says (chap. 37). Bulstrode unhappily is forced to associate Ladislaw directly with Raffles's presence in the town and tries to buy him off, as if in danger of blackmail from this quarter also. "It was the first time he had encountered an open expression of scorn from any man higher than Raffles"; but after talking with Ladislaw the banker comforts himself with the reflection that he, at least, is not likely to "publish" their conversation (chap. 61). Later Ladislaw remarks to Lydgate that he is surprised gossip has not accused him of plotting "with Raffles to murder Bulstrode" (chap. 79). There is no getting around the fact that this stranger poses a certain threat from the past to Casaubon, also, and that he is the first to inform Dorothea of her husband's inadequate scholarship (chap. 21). Dorothea Casaubon scorns Mrs. Cadwallader's comparison of Will to an Italian with white mice. For her "he was a creature who entered into every one's feelings, and could take the pressure of their thought instead of urging his own with iron resistance" (chap. 50). The contrast is with her husband, and the terms—"entered into every one's feelings"—describe a welcome intrusion: Ladislaw and Raffles are entirely unlike personalities, the one antithetical to the other. Yet both bear information against some of the Middlemarchers.

Raffles figures most importantly in the novel not as a character but as a catalyst in the drama of information and circumstances. It may be better to disregard him as a person altogether and concentrate on the reaction taking place around him. As George Eliot and her commentators have been careful to point out, the threads of connection run this way and that in *Middlemarch*; the very process of the novel's composition from multiple actions signals that connections and parallels, however slight, can usually be found. There are no true limits to the actions of circumstance, which extend indiscernibly backward and forward in time; and a reality so construed invites ironic overstatement of the particular turnings it takes. An event that can be identified as anything approaching a beginning can be expected to be very slight, and in a just narrative of circumstances ought to be the slightest and most inconspicuous circumstance of all. Yet the information that identifies that circumstance and enables blackmail, that threatens to connect various narratives within the narrative as a whole, craves notice as a melodramatic beginning. Some such contradictory desiderata inspire the improbable narrative in chapters 12 and 13 of *Felix Holt*, in which a practical joke, lost pocketbook, stubbed toe, heroic reticence, and matching information deliberately overstate the odds against discovery in order to apologize, as it were, for narrating the beginning of the main action. To introduce Raffles and the blackmail action in *Middlemarch*, George Eliot does something quite similar—in shorter compass, with much greater finesse, and with shrewd reference to her theme of knowledge.

Chapter 41 of the novel is the deliberate introduction of a line of suspense, in the course of which we see a little more of Joshua Rigg—the least important stranger to Middlemarch—and a representative action of the new character, John Raffles, attempting to extort a little money from

Rigg. There is a certain amount of exposition concerning the past relation of the two men and the tobacco shop belonging to Rigg's mother in a seaport town. The epigraph from the clown's song in *Twelfth Night*—"By swaggering could I never thrive. / For the rain it raineth every day"—describes Raffles, who is said to have "the air of a swaggerer" and wishes to pass as "having been educated at an academy." The complete song would seem to reflect on Raffles's aging, his unflattering sexual relation to Rigg's mother, and his propensity to drink. But all of the really useful exposition is compassed by the words at the opening and closing of the chapter that introduce the line of suspense, hint at the main action in which Raffles will be involved, and mysteriously concern writing. The opening paragraph is a single sentence informing us that Bulstrode and Rigg—now bearing the name Featherstone and occupying Stone Court—have in the course of business exchanged "a letter or two." The second paragraph consists of the following digression:

> Who shall tell what may be the effect of writing? If it happens to have been cut in stone, though it lie face downmost for ages on a forsaken beach, or "rest quietly under the drums and tramplings of many conquests," it may end by letting us into the secret of usurpations and other scandals gossiped about long empires ago,—this world being apparently a huge whispering-gallery. Such conditions are often minutely represented in our petty life-times. As the stone which has been kicked by generations of clowns may come by curious little links of effect under the eyes of a scholar, through whose labours it may at last fix the date of invasions and unlock religions, so a bit of ink and paper which has long been an innocent wrapping or stop-gap may at last be laid open under the one pair of eyes which have knowledge enough to turn it into the opening of a catastrophe. To Uriel watching the progress of planetary history from the sun, the one result would be just as much of a coincidence as the other.
>
> (chap. 41)

The digression is one of mock solemnity and superb irony, and of economy that can fully be appreciated only by reading *Felix Holt* and *Middlemarch* entire. The subject, "the effect of writing," is developed by analogy between any scrap of paper and inscriptions in stone that through time may become archaeological discoveries, and by simultaneous comparison between writing and speech—specifically gossip or whispering. A quotation from Sir Thomas Browne's *Urne-Burial* announces the theme of time and accident, suggests the fragility of evidence for entire lifetimes in the past, and promises an exposition both scientific and fantastic. As opposed to gossip then or now, writing may occur at one time and be read at another, and as evidence may therefore both conceal secrets and reveal them. With her fine metaphysical image of the whispering gallery George Eliot elaborates this difference: one can actually construct a reliable means to deliver gossip across a large space, as in a whispering gallery; paradoxically, the more permanent record of writing is subject over time to greater effect of chance. Cause and effect have long been featured in the novelist's moral and historical teaching, but the "curious little links of effect" preserving a decipherable stone or paper are oddly diminished; instead of a formidable operation of cause and effect it is the element of chance that brings access to information. The placing of the writing "under the one pair of eyes which have knowledge enough to turn it into the opening of a catastrophe" recalls precisely what happened in *Felix Holt*, in the elaborate series of chances that placed the appropriate bit of writing under Rufus Lyon's eyes; because the eyes are those of "a scholar" and the ancient writing may "unlock religions," a more immediate reference is to the wrong Key of Edward Casaubon. Reduction of "the secret of usurpations" to "other scandals" and the contrast of "long empires ago" with "our own petty lifetimes" have been implicit in the antiromantic thesis of George Eliot's realism since *Adam Bede*, but here the comparisons have to do with information and with writing in particular. In the full context of *Middlemarch*, moreover, we understand the comparison between evidence of use to archaeologists, who are third parties to usurpations and scandals of the ancient world, and evidence of use to blackmailers, who are third parties to stories of the more recent past. Both kinds of agents need only information to become informants.

The comparisons ironically exalt blackmailers at the expense of scholars, in fact, but thus far the novelist is not telling what the low writing consists of. In her opening paragraph she has hinted that it is a letter, and in the closing sentence of the chapter she specifies "a letter signed *Nicholas Bulstrode*," but this careful withholding of information through the course of the chapter later appears as still greater overstatement, since the paper does not turn out to be an incriminating letter at all, but merely evidence to Raffles's eyes—which "have knowledge enough," like the scholar's— that Bulstrode is in Middlemarch. The signature at the close no doubt suggests the real subject of the chapter, but the reader does not yet know enough of Bulstrode's past to connect it, even by analogy, to the sleazy past of the new character, Raffles. The digression itself contains a hint in the reference to Uriel, from whose perspective on the sun a catastrophe induced by a bit of paper and ink cannot be distinguished from a discovery important to history. The allusion to Uriel adumbrates a fall for someone, while in effect apologizing for the narrative suspense, since even angels lack foreknowledge of the plot. The archangel Uriel, stationed on the sun in *Paradise Lost*, encountered Satan on his way to earth and even pointed the way, because he could not penetrate Satan's intentions. The "false dissembler" goes unperceived:

> For neither Man nor Angel can discern
> Hypocrisy, the only evil that walks
> Invisible, except to God alone,
> By his permissive will, through Heav'n and Earth
> [*Paradise Lost* 3.682–85]

Since Bulstrode is a hypocrite and one who expressly believes that he walks invisible by God's permissive will, the allusion seems pointed.

As we later understand, just because Bulstrode has continued to walk invisible, he has concluded that he is favored with a special Providence. When he first encounters Raffles in person, therefore, the difference between "spiritual relations and conceptions of divine purposes" and the prospect of public exposure of his story is marked:

> Five minutes before, the expanse of his life had been submerged in its evening sunshine which shone backward to its remembered morning: sin seemed to be a question of doctrine and inward penitence, humiliation an exercise of the closet, the bearing of his deeds a matter of private vision adjusted solely by spiritual relations and conceptions of the divine purposes. And now, as if by some hideous magic, this loud red figure had risen before him in unmanageable solidity,—an incorporate past which had not entered into his imagination of chastisements.
>
> (chap. 53)

Suddenly it is Raffles who is the devil, and it is clear why George Eliot has chosen Bulstrode as the exemplary victim of modern blackmail. Her purpose is not to whip a form of hypocrisy that is peculiarly distasteful to her, still less to belittle evangelical Christianity or its Puritan forebears. Rather, she writes as the novelist of a secular age, conscious of belief and unbelief. She chooses Bulstrode, in her own providential gesture as novelist, in order to argue that if divine Omniscience is no longer a plausible threat to behavior, then the fortuitous knowledge of blackmailers may take its place. Her choice of Bulstrode, with his outdated religious pretensions, may have been learned from Hawthorne's Puritan subjects; and the "loud red figure" of Raffles, who rationally conceived incorporates merely the "past," serves ambiguously as the Devil had served before him, both to persecute the victim and to share the blame.

Blackmailers, after all, can shore up the inward conscience with the outward demands of society: to be private is no longer, in the nineteenth century, assuredly to be alone with God, and therefore to be private is not wholly in the interest of society. "It was an hour of anguish for [Bulstrode] very different from the hours in which his struggle had been securely private, and which had ended with a sense that his secret misdeeds were pardoned and his services accepted. Those misdeeds even when committed—had they not been half sanctified by the singleness of his desire to devote himself and all he possessed to the furtherance of the divine scheme?" But the test of deeds and of devotion is no longer divine but social. Blackmail poses the threat of shame rather than conscience, and the threat therefore strikes deepest at the career that is a secular legacy of Puritanism: "For who would understand the work within him? Who would not, when there was the pretext of casting disgrace upon him, confound his whole life and the truths he had espoused, in one heap of obloquy?" (chap. 53). Later on, in a franker statement about Bulstrode's "misdeeds," a statement less in the indirect style, George Eliot will imply that a belief in Omniscience has never been a sufficient check to behavior, since many misdeeds are "like the subtle muscular movements which are not taken account of in the consciousness . . . and it is only what we are vividly conscious of that we can vividly imagine to be seen by Omniscience" (chap. 68). A blackmailer, as opposed to a personal conscience, usually hints pretty clearly what he has seen, and he may even exaggerate a little.

Chapter 41 does not yet give us Bulstrode directly, only the scrap of paper that Raffles uses to wedge his flask in its leather cover and on which he eventually discovers the name of the banker. The story we are given instead is that of Raffles, "a man obviously on the way towards sixty, very florid and hairy," who has become the second companion to the frog-featured woman who is Joshua Rigg's mother, a parasite of the tobacco shop and of the mother's income from the frog-faced son. George Eliot's original readers could not foresee the eerie resemblance to the short-lived ambition of Tracy in the tobacco shop of Hitchcock's *Blackmail*; and readers of *Middlemarch* for the first time still cannot foresee the parallel with Bulstrode's earlier life as the second husband to the pawnbroker's wife, whose daughter married the son of Casaubon's aunt; or the way in which Bulstrode has also thrived at the expense of an absent child, who became Will Ladislaw's mother. The air of prostitution, much filtered when Bulstrode's story is later given directly, is heavy in chapter 41. "Having made this rather lofty comparison" between ancient and modern inscriptions and their results, the narrator comes down, "I am less uneasy in calling attention to the existence of low people by whose interference, however little we may like it, the course of the world is very much determined." Something might be done "by not lightly giving occasion to their existence," she says—alluding to the sexual transaction that produced the "superfluity" who is Joshua Rigg. "But those who, like Peter Featherstone, never had a copy of themselves demanded, are the very last to wait for such a request either in prose or verse" (chap. 41). The riposte of George Eliot's own prose is very skillful, the play on "copy" bowing toward the preceding paragraph on "the effect of writing" but also glancing back to the "copy of himself" that Mr. Casaubon has not achieved, having "not yet succeeded in issuing copies of his mythological key" (chap. 29). But just as there is indignation about Casaubon's impotence beneath the surface of *Middlemarch*, there is scarcely concealed contempt for unattractive sexuality associated with the woman who is Rigg's mother and Raffles's paramour. The failure of monogamy and ugliness of motive parallel Bulstrode's history. After Raffles has returned to Middlemarch and begun to blackmail Bulstrode, the latter's past returns to him, "only the pleasures of it seeming to have lost their quality." The scathing commentary on low people in chapter 41 prepares for the sexual suggestion in the description of Bulstrode's terror: memory "smarting like a reopened wound," or "a still quivering part of himself, bringing shudders and bitter flavours and the tinglings of a merited shame." Bulstrode recalls privately "shrinking" from the very business of pawnbroking (chap. 61). If there is a prostitute in Bulstrode's past, however, it is not a frog-faced woman but Bulstrode himself.

George Eliot is now working at a great distance from the initial experience of her own secret, the affair with Lewes and pseudonymous authorship; yet both kinds of secret are present when Raffles appears on the scene in *Middlemarch*. Though it is difficult to speak of shame in any form without recourse to sexual language, it is fair to say that disreputable sexual relations play a distinct part in the small group of characters around Raffles and in the group in Bulstrode's past, and therefore in Ladislaw's ancestry. More evidently the digression on writing in chapter 41, in the inscription in stone "which has been kicked by generations of clowns" but to the eyes of a scholar may "fix the date of invasions and unlock religions," recalls George Eliot's other secret. In the course of the Liggins episode in 1859 Charles Bray had defended C. Holte Bracebridge, the most officious investigator of the novelist's identity, on the ground that, as an archaeologist, Bracebridge was simply acting "in the way of his profession." George Eliot replied with acerbity, in the same letter in which she defended secrets and repudiated "the assumption of entire knowingness," that she was "not yet an 'archäological' subject." The same spirit is apparent in the fine irony that compares the evidence of scholarship to the "bit of ink and paper" of use to a blackmailer. The digression that begins "Who shall tell what may be the effect of writing?" is her introduction of Raffles and his low relations. Insofar as the question is about the experience of writing, it is answered most fully in the chapter that immediately follows, which has nothing to do with Raffles or Bulstrode.

Chapter 42 addresses the nearness of Edward Casaubon's death, from Casaubon's own point of view. In an extended soliloquy, uncharacteristic of *Middlemarch*, he foresees Dorothea's marriage to Ladislaw; and the bitter part of Dorothea in this chapter is to discover the depth of her own resentment of her husband's alienation from her. Yet the background for these dramatic moments is authorship; and the cause of alienation is authorship, for it is Dorothea's opinion of him as a scholar rather than her possible unfaithfulness that Casaubon has come to fear. A fantasy of "triumphant authorship"—he is thinking of Carp and company—modulates toward the indignant prediction of Ladislaw's succession via the "jealousy and vindictiveness" of his situation as a writer. It is not primarily "the autumnal unripeness of his authorship," his failure to complete his work before now, that informs Casaubon's fears and poisons his relation to Dorothea, but an "uneasy susceptibility" inherent in "some kinds of authorship";

Mr. Casaubon was now brooding over something through which the question of his health and life haunted his silence with a more harassing importunity even than through the autumnal unripeness of his authorship. It is true that this might be called his central ambition; but there are some kinds of authorship in which by far the largest result is the uneasy susceptibility accumulated in the consciousness of the author,—one knows of the river by a few streaks amid a long-gathered deposit of uncomfortable mud. That was the way with Mr. Casaubon's hard, intellectual labours. Their most characteristic result was not the "Key to all Mythologies," but a morbid consciousness that others did not give him the place which he had not demonstrably merited,—a perpetual, suspicious conjecture that the views entertained of him were not to his advantage,—a melancholy absence of passion in his efforts at achievement, and a passionate resistance to the confession that he had achieved nothing.

Clearly such "kinds of authorship" attach to kinds of personality, as the syntax of the last sentence begins to insist. But the necessary condition of this terrible alienation is authorship itself: the distance between writer and readers, the divorce of intellectual effort and result. The subject here is a special form of consciousness, and it is not hard to guess that George Eliot is drawing partly on her own experience. In her following paragraph she translates susceptibility as "no security against wounds" (chap. 42).

Therefore the question addressed to writing when Raffles is first introduced to the novel, the subject of scholarship of the ancient past, and even the indirect allusion to urn-burial have to do also with the experience of Casaubon, he of the "lifeless embalmment of knowledge," whose own death is now rapidly approaching and who will attempt to affect the future through a codicil to his will. Writing and scholarship are closely associated in *Middlemarch* with consciousness itself. Scholars cannot help but be aware of the sometimes tangential bearing of evidence upon the conclusions that they shape in narrative form, which are then published and await uncertain reception. Writers are engaged in a practice that is inherently discontinuous, acutely aware of the distance between inward feeling and the outward result of their being. The silence of the print culture is not pure silence but seething with information, and with attendant anxieties of inference and reputation. Hence the figure for Casaubon's "consciousness of authorship" draws briefly on geology to represent a temporal discontinuity—"one knows of the river by a few streaks amid the long-gathered deposit of uncomfortable mud." Note that the formation of consciousness can only be inferred from the evidence, which is as scientific and as chancy as the evidence of inscriptions on stone or of ink on paper. The figure is mischievously oblique. What reader ever supposed that Casaubon's mind resembled a river? One knows there must have been a river, however, because an uncomfortable consciousness remains, just as one knows there have been authors when one finds a lot of print.

It is evident that "consciousness" is of increasing interest to George Eliot—she uses the word itself with increasing frequency in the later novels. By studying the projection and displacements of *Romola,* one can deduce that consciousness requires a degree of doubleness like that which the heroine regrets in Savonarola or contemns in Tito. Consciousness assumes identity of the self over time, yet a life that is in fact single and continuous cannot always see itself very well. Doubleness and discontinuity enable greater consciousness—once the connections have been made. And if consciousness does not develop of itself, shaming may contribute to the process: in *Felix Holt,* because of her secret past, Mrs. Transome has far more consciousness than Harold Transome, but "outside conscience" or shame comes to Harold's assistance. Vivid consciousness is likely to occur when a discontinuous life is revisited—when the life is not strung out year after year, as it were, but doubled back upon itself, year against year. Thus blackmailers may positively enhance consciousness. Of many implicit definitions of "consciousness" in George Eliot's later work, one of the finest—which brilliantly focuses all these considerations—is a striking image for Bulstrode's state of mind after the return of Raffles:

> Into this second life Bulstrode's past had now risen, only the pleasures of it seeming to have lost their quality. Night and day, without interruption save of brief sleep which only wove retrospect and fear into a fantastic present, he felt the scenes of his earlier life coming between him and everything else, as obstinately as when we look through the window from a lighted room, the objects we turn our backs on are still before us, instead of the grass and the trees. The successive events inward and outward were there in one view: though each might be dwelt on in turn, the rest still kept their hold in the consciousness.
>
> (chap. 61)

Such consciousness, superimposing "inward and outward" events and occluding a pastoral alternative, results in this case from the experience of being blackmailed.

Blackmail is the stuff of sensation novels, and it is no wonder that students of George Eliot have had difficulty in accommodating the story of Bulstrode to their interpretations of *Middlemarch,* which is nothing like a sensation novel as a whole. The first requirement of such accommodation is to accept Bulstrode's close relation to Lydgate, and by contiguities and partial analogies to other characters in the novel as well. Still, the manifest ambition of the novel to become an epic of society might seem to preclude such crass irony as may be imported by a ruinous bit of information. Like Fielding before her, George Eliot aspired to an epic representation of contemporary life, but her model was finally Dante's epic rather than Homer's. The historical particularity of Dante's characters appealed to her nineteenth-century sense of past and present. The urgency of his dead heroes' longing to establish a link with this world she reinterpreted as a common experience of discontinuity within the world. Her Casaubon identifies himself almost complacently as a ghost: "I feed too much on the inward sources; I live too much with the dead. My mind is something like the ghost of an ancient" (chap. 2). Fame is no less a need for Casaubon than it was for one of Dante's characters, and his apparent complacency turns to anguish as George Eliot enlarges his story and makes it representative of a modern experience of writing in which she shared. But for a character with one life irrevocably fixed in the past and another life in the present, she chose Bulstrode, and arranged things so that the information threatening Bulstrode's career threatened Lydgate's as well.

The Dantean model first inspired Mrs. Transome in *Felix Holt,* a woman whose history actually anticipates Lydgate's modern experience. Like Lydgate, Mrs. Transome "had been thought wonderfully clever and accomplished, and had been rather ambitious of intellectual superiority" in her youth; and she has since experienced "crosses, mortifications, money-cares, conscious blameworthiness" (chap. 1). Yet the promise of her youth is never given a chance to impress the reader, as Lydgate's impresses. It is he whose stature and whose punishment are most Dantean of all—though his life is scarcely as divided as Bulstrode's. The stories of Lydgate and Bulstrode together combine the pursuit of knowledge with the constraint of public opinion, in the one case elaborating the novelist's most careful study of the action of circumstances and in the other melodramatically and metaphorically demonstrating the effect of discontinuity, and of "successive events inward and outward" as they obstinately return from the window of a lighted room.

Power as Partiality in *Middlemarch*

Patricia McKee

Dorothea Brooke, the heroine of *Middlemarch,* has as uneasy an effect on the world around her as do Richardson's Pamela and Clarissa. She, too, is hard to take and difficult to place, and, as in Clarissa's case, the difficulty is initially posed as a problem of "marriageability."

> And how should Dorothea not marry?—a girl so handsome and with such prospects? Nothing could hinder it but her love of extremes, and her insistence on regulating life according to notions which might cause a wary man to hesitate before he made her an offer, or even might lead her at last to refuse all offers. A young lady of some birth and fortune, who knelt suddenly down on a brick floor by the side of a sick labourer and prayed fervidly as if she thought herself living in the time of the Apostles—who had strange whims of fasting like a Papist, and of sitting up at night to read old theological books!

Loving extremes, Dorothea seems unlikely to be accepted as, or accepting of, a match. The problem is not only that her excesses threaten to make her unacceptable. The difficulty also lies in the fact that she does not want a "match." Sir James Chettam is unthinkable as a husband for Dorothea precisely because he is so agreeable: "an amiable handsome baronet, who said 'Exactly' to her remarks even when she expressed uncertainty—how could he affect her as a lover?"

From *Heroic Commitment in Richardson, Eliot and James.* © 1986 by Princeton University Press.

Dorothea's desire is not a desire to be met but a desire to be exceeded by something larger than herself.

> Her mind was theoretic, and yearned by its nature after some lofty conception of the world which might frankly include the parish of Tipton and her own rule of conduct there; she was enamoured of intensity and greatness, and rash in embracing whatever seemed to her to have those aspects; likely to seek martyrdom, to make retractations, and then to incur martyrdom after all in a quarter where she had not sought it.

Theoretic rather than realistic, Dorothea desires an idea rather than an object and marries, in Casaubon, an ideal rather than a man. This is a mistake, a mistake due to her idealistic yearnings; but the narrative does not resolve the mistake in realistic terms. For Dorothea turns around and marries, in Will Ladislaw, a second husband who is also more an idea than a man. This is not so much the fault of Dorothea, perhaps, as of George Eliot, who simply never, as critics point out, presents Ladislaw as a convincingly realistic character. But if Ladislaw is considered a failure on George Eliot's part, he is a "failure" congruent with Dorothea's own need to idealize characters.

Middlemarch insists, however, that we reconsider our sense of both failure and success. Dorothea's theoretic mind may imply her alienation, since ideas are not men; and in this the novel may seem realistic. Georg Lukács, for example, identifies the form of the realistic novel with the form of human desire that seeks satisfaction in a world inadequate to satisfy it. As in the Freudian reality principle, human desire and the real world are discovered to be incommensurable. *Middlemarch,* however, though it discovers such incommensurability, affirms it rather than identifying it with frustration. If Dorothea is typical of heroes and heroines in that she does not settle for things as they are and, like Saint Theresa, to whom she is compared, sees the world in unrealistic terms, she also, like Theresa, has an "unrealistic" power to change things into something different. This is clear, for example, in the effect she has on Will Ladislaw:

> He felt, when he parted from her, that the brief words by which he had tried to convey to her his feeling . . . would only profit by their brevity when Dorothea had to interpret them; he felt that in her mind he had found his highest estimate.

Those who respond to Dorothea's power thus become something different, and something more, than they are in themselves. Her power is not, then, a matter of assuming control over others but a process of becoming part of others and so changing and extending the meaning of both herself and others. Thus her power is generative rather than controlling of meaning; and it in fact depends on her own and others' willingness to "let go" of meaning. As the above passage suggests, Will does not control or even know the part of his meaning that lies in her mind. But his increase of value depends on allowing his meaning to go out of bounds and out of his possession. What he is in himself and what he is in Dorothea are in these ways incommensurable. But the incommensurability constitutes an increase, not a loss.

This is the relation with the world for which Dorothea yearns. But it is an unsettling relation, unsettling because it demands that meaning be allowed to exceed knowledge and possession. If in the above passage, for example, Dorothea interprets Ladislaw's words to have a meaning he does not even know, it is difficult to say whether the meaning belongs to him or her. Thus we, confronted with such meaning, cannot say who means it. Dorothea's authority to create meaning—like the authority of Pamela and Clarissa—is an authority that is not exactly her own: it is dependent on others and inseparable from such dependence, a matter of corresponding differences rather than of control. More explicitly in *Middlemarch* than in Richardson's novels, however, the interdependence and indeterminacy of meaning which result demand that knowledge and determination be given up. Rather than learning to acknowledge reality, Dorothea learns to deny the limits that knowledge imposes on experience. She proceeds according to the belief that things can be different because she believes them to be different. And the narrator works with her in this. For the narrative consistently evades and undermines knowledge, insisting that we cannot know all that is meaningful but that we can make room for it if we do not limit ourselves to knowledge.

The narrative itself thus becomes hard to take at its word. The narrator is always conscious of the misrepresentation of any representation and insists on the incommensurability of representation and reality and the incommensurability of different representations. Her prose often exceeds the bounds of logical representation and thus precludes any understanding that would determine meaning. On the other hand, the narrator often is difficult to understand not because she gives us indeterminate prose but because, in another sense, she represents as meaningful something that we are accustomed to view as a loss of meaning. Perhaps the most familiar example of the difficulty readers have accepting her words at face value is the resistance they tend to feel to the conclusion of the novel. The narrator insists that Dorothea gets what she wants:

> No life would have been possible to Dorothea which was not
> filled with emotion, and she had now a life filled also with a
> beneficient activity which she had not the doubtful pains of dis-
> covering and marking out for herself. . . . Dorothea could have
> liked nothing better, since wrongs existed, than that her hus-
> band should be in the thick of a struggle against them, and that
> she should give him wifely help. Many who knew her, thought
> it a pity that so substantive and rare a creature should have been
> absorbed into the life of another, and be only known in a cer-
> tain circle as a wife and mother. But no one stated exactly what
> else that was in her power she ought rather to have done.

"Absorbed into the life of another," Dorothea has achieved what she
wished for at the beginning of the novel: to be part of something larger
than her own life. That this incommensurable relation of self and world is
difficult to accept as fulfillment is recognized by the narrator's reference to
those characters who cannot accept it as such. In order to accept what the
narrator is saying about Dorothea, we must recognize that those characters
"who knew her" are incapable of accepting what she is. It is knowledge
that fails here as Dorothea succeeds, for knowledge fails to make room for
the incommensurable differences she values.

The problem here, then, is not that others do not get to know Dorothea. The problem is that we do not recognize the value of the unknow-
able. Dorothea's effect on the world is "incalculably diffusive" and thus
cannot be known because knowledge is a matter of calculation and determination. Yet knowledge is also, therefore, an interpretation of reality; it
is one limited representation among other possible interpretations, such as
the narrator's own. One of the means Eliot uses to insist on the indeterminacy of meaning in *Middlemarch* is her recognition that meaning is always
a matter of interpretation. It is a major concern of the narrative to represent not only what happens to characters but how other characters interpret what happens. And the multiple interpretations undermine the possibility of knowledge, even though knowledge, as in the above passage, is
claimed by some. Those who know Dorothea always identify her, however, in terms that place her out of bounds. She is known as someone who
cannot be understood, for example. Thus the only way to know or determine her meaning is to determine it as excessive. The terms of knowledge,
therefore, exclude her from knowledge, but in doing so they also claim to
define her and to limit her meaning by ruling it out of bounds. It is because of the exclusive terms of knowledgeable interpretation that Eliot insists that it is a particularly inadequate interpretation.

The only way to represent Dorothea's meaning as significant is to represent her in indeterminate terms. This is what the narrative does. I will be considering in this chapter how the narrator's commitment to indeterminate meaning that exceeds the bounds of knowledge revises our conceptions of truth, of power, and of authority. Insisting that none of these phenomena is itself knowable, because they really exceed the orderly limits of knowledge, Eliot also insists that none of them be considered a matter of control. Like Dorothea's power, the narrator's power does not impose limits on meaning but attempts to open up the possibilities of meaning. Doing this, she insists on the increased potential of meaning, for such meaning is always subject to change. In order to indicate the mutual concerns of Dorothea and her narrator, I will consider the excesses they have in common. From the very beginning of the narrative, Dorothea is represented by the narrator in terms that allow for her excesses; and thus Eliot suggests an alternative to other characters' interpretations of Dorothea's behavior that rule out those excesses.

Consistently interpreted as outside the bounds of proper behavior, Dorothea is unacceptable at times because she gets carried away and goes too far, and at other times because she falls short of the standards of propriety. As the prelude puts it, her behavior is seen alternately as "extravagance" and "lapse" by those around her. Kneeling on laborers' floors and fasting might be interpreted with equal ease either way. But whichever way Dorothea is interpreted, she is too much to take. Her excesses and others' responses to them suggest again Geoffrey Hartman's "redundancy principle," cited in the chapter on *Pamela* [elsewhere]. Hartman's thesis that poetic language is indeterminate emphasizes that its excesses can be read in two ways: "Poetry either says too much—approaches the inexpressible—or too little—approaches the inexpressive." On whichever side one sees it, there is always an excess, and this is what "allows, if it does not actually compel, interpretation." Such meaning demands interpretation, but it precludes knowledge. Dorothea's behavior is similarly excessive, indeterminate, and demanding. But others do not respond to that demand, for it demands too much: that her meaning depends on them and thus that they take part in uncertain meaning.

We are not accustomed to seeing people as poems, of course, nor is the world of *Middlemarch,* which tends to interpret Dorothea as without worth because she exceeds determinate worth. With no more practical use than a poem, Dorothea is responded to by other characters with some version of Mrs. Cadwallader's " 'I throw her over.' " Impractical and unrealistic, she is identified with waste because there is nothing to be done with her. But Will Ladislaw's insistence to her that " 'You *are* a poem' " suggests that the difficulty of saying what she is is a difficulty crucial to her extraordinary value. Clearly, for Ladislaw, Dorothea's excesses do not exceed but extend the bounds of meaning to include "incalculably diffusive" effects. Dorothea's excesses, like the excesses of poetic language, are what make her meaningful, precisely because her meaning is incalculable: indeterminate and changeable.

"Likely to seek martyrdom, to make retractions, and then to incur martyrdom after all in a quarter where she had not sought it," Dorothea is repeatedly "martyred" not because she is "true" to certain beliefs but because she is inconsistent, not true at all if truth is unchanging. She will seek martyrdom by sacrificing her youth and intensity to Casaubon, regret it, then sacrifice her estate to marry Will Ladislaw. She will "be spoken of to a younger generation as a fine girl who married a sickly clergyman, old enough to be her father, and in little more than a year after his death gave up her estate to marry his cousin—young enough to have been his son, with no property, and not well-born." From this point of view, Dorothea does not "get" anywhere; rather, she proceeds by veering from one extreme to the other, neither of which is satisfactory in others' eyes. According to the gossip of Middlemarch, "she could not have been 'a nice woman,' else she would not have married either the one or the other." Inconsistent but also repetitive from this point of view, Dorothea's marriages go too far in opposite directions to be acceptable. She is outside the bounds of propriety either way, having missed the happy mean of proper behavior.

If in this case she goes too far, in other cases she does not go far enough to be acceptable. In the first scene of the novel, Celia asks Dorothea to divide with her the jewels left them by their mother. Indifferent to the jewelry on religious principles, Dorothea at first seeks a sort of martyrdom by giving up all claim to them. But she retracts when she sees the emeralds, which are the best pieces in the collection. She puts them on, "all the while . . . trying to justify her delight in the colours by merging them in her mystic religious joy." The merger, however, is not successful in Celia's eyes: "she repeated to herself that Dorothea was inconsistent: either she should have taken her full share of the jewels, or, after what she had said, she would have renounced them altogether." Dorothea, who does neither, thus incurs an unlooked-for martyrdom, subject to Celia's interpretation that she has things both ways in her effort to combine her mixed feelings rather than choose between them. Here again, she gets nowhere. She is wrong both at the beginning and the end, and, in addition, her behavior lacks resolution because she cannot carry through either alternative but tries to combine them. In order to satisfy Celia, Dorothea would have to do one thing or the other. Yet she remains in between the two alternatives that Celia sees as mutually exclusive. She takes part of the jewels, so beautiful that her pleasure in them may be merged with religious feeling, and thus allows herself part of both the jewels and the religious joy.

In the case of the marriages, Dorothea's alterations go too far; she lacks any middle ground. In the case of the jewels, her sense of alternatives seems itself to be lacking, so that she falls short of proper distinctions, in the midst of undistinguished differences. In both instances, whether going too far or falling short of the boundaries of proper meaning, her behavior seems redundant. Others cannot make sense of her because she does things that do not fit together, either logically or chronologically. She is inconsistent, and she does not get anywhere with others, because one action neither agrees with nor leads to the next.

But to Dorothea's disparities are added the disparities of others, for in both cases it is others' interpretation that make her behavior unsatisfactory. Differences in her own behavior are compounded by differences between her self and her beholders as the narrative shifts among differing points of view. Others' interpretations make distinctions where Dorothea does not; their distinctions are exclusive, and her sense of difference is inclusive. Yet the representation of her husbands as one "old enough to be her father" and the other "young enough to have been his son" suggests that exclusive distinctions are more a matter of representation than reality. For one might say that Casaubon is old enough to be her father and Ladislaw is her own age. But then Dorothea would not be represented as consistently out of bounds; she would be even more difficult to place. Exclusive distinctions enable representation to avoid such confusions. But the representation of distinctions avoids the reality that the narrator is attempting to represent: a reality in which differences and inconsistencies abound without being contained by the limits of clear distinction and agreement. The clarification of differences depends on representations that the narrator is unwilling to make with any consistency.

The prelude to the novel prepares us for this when comparing modern women to the martyr Saint Theresa. The description insists on their similarities but also insists that the difference between them is the difference between agreement and difference themselves. Modern women are different because of the irreconcilable disparities in their lives:

> Many Theresas have been born who found for themselves no
> epic life wherein there was a constant unfolding of far-resonant
> action; perhaps only a life of mistakes, the offspring of a certain

> spiritual grandeur ill-matched with the meanness of opportunity; perhaps a tragic failure which found no sacred poet and sank unwept into oblivion. With dim lights and tangled circumstance they tried to shape their thought and deed in noble agreement; but after all, to common eyes their struggles seemed mere inconsistency and formlessness; for these later-born Theresas were helped by no coherent social faith and order which could perform the function of knowledge for the ardently willing soul. Their ardour alternated between a vague ideal and the common yearning of womanhood; so that the one was disapproved as extravagance, and the other condemned as a lapse.

Such lives are unfitting and "ill-matched": formless, without coherence, without agreement between spirit and opportunity or thought and deed. The inability to find any object or objective that meets the subjects' spiritual grandeur is due to multiple causes: to circumstances, to others' interpretations, and to the lack of anything that functions as knowledge. Because they do not *know,* such women not only lack the means of integrating thought and action but also lack the means of knowing whether such integrity is possible. With no fitting object for their ardor, they shift between two incommensurable relations to the world. In one, ardor goes too far to be suitable to others, as in Dorothea's rejection of all the jewels according to a "vague ideal." In the other, ardor falls short of suitability to others, as when she takes only the best emeralds in "common yearning" for their beauty.

The alternating behavior of such women and the alternative interpretations of their behavior by others, both of which contribute to the confusion of their experience, are reflected in the prose of the passage. The narrator, like the women she describes, is involved in "irreconcilable disparities" which are represented as shifting alternatives rather than resolved differences. Nothing provides coherence: not the individual, nor her society, nor those who observe her, nor the narrator. For, like Dorothea in her marriage or in the scene with the jewels, the narrator alternates among rather than choosing between alternatives. We are told, for example, that for any of the possible kinds of failure, there are different explanations: others do not understand such women, and they themselves do not know what they are doing. If we want to choose between these alternative explanations, we are not allowed to do so. For the sentence actually says that others do not understand these women *because* they themselves do not know what they are doing, making the alternative explanations dependent on each other.

With dim lights and tangled circumstance they tried to shape their thought and deed in noble agreement; but after all, to common eyes their struggles seemed mere inconsistency and formlessless; for these later-born Theresas were helped by no coherent social faith and order which could perform the function of knowledge for the ardently willing soul.

This is not logical; the three statements do not fit together to give us a clear sense of causality. They seem to be out of order, and we thereby alternate among explanations rather than distinguishing specific causes and effects. The prose itself is redundant: it either says too little or says too much to be knowledgeable.

We can read the prelude, therefore, as about the narrator as well as about her heroine. For the narrator, too, finds in her narrative "no epic life wherein there was a constant unfolding of far-resonant action"; and her efforts, too, often seem "mere inconsistency and formlessness," as in this passage. She represent meaning by a process that shifts meaning: from one point of view to another, from one point in time to another, and among all points so that they cannot be seen as points of a logical progression. The narrator's authority will not be used in *Middlemarch* to impose order. It will instead authorize the recognition of incommensurable differences whose representation exceeds the bounds of orderly prose. The project of the narrator, as her prose suggests, is not to create an alternative form of secure meaning that can take the place of knowledge. It is to insist on the greater significance of meaning that includes insecure and "undistinguished" differences; and so, including multiple alternatives, it precludes an alternative order.

Chronology

1819   Mary Anne Evans born November 22 on the Arbury estate, Warwickshire, to Robert Evans, carpenter and estate agent, and his wife, Christiana Pearson Evans, daughter of a yeoman farmer.

1824–35   Educated first at a local dame school, then at boarding schools in Attleborough, Nuneaton, and Coventry. In 1832, she witnesses the election riot caused by the first Reform Bill.

1836   Death of mother. Evans and elder sister take over management of the household.

1837   Marriage of elder sister; household management now in Evans's hands. Studies Italian, German, and music under tutors.

1838   Visits London for the first time with her brother Isaac. Schooling has made Evans a zealous Evangelical. Returns to father's house.

1841   Evans and her father move to Coventry. Reads Charles Hennell's *Inquiry into the Origins of Christianity* and Bray's *The Philosophy of Necessity*. Converted from Evangelical Christianity to "a crude state of free-thinking."

1842   Refuses to attend church with her father; later returns to Coventry and to church (although not to her old beliefs).

1843–44   Stays with Dr. and Mrs. Brabant at Devizes. Works on a translation of Strauss's *Das Leben Jesu*. Leaves precipitously, probably at the insistence of Mrs. Brabant, because of her strong admiration for the elderly intellectual Dr. Brabant. Returns to Coventry, and continues work on the translation (published 1846).

1845   Rejects marriage proposal from artist friend. Teaches herself Hebrew.

1849	Death of father. Begins translation of Spinoza's *Tractatus Theologico-Politicus*. Travels to Geneva, where she remains until 1850.
1850–53	Returns to England, becomes assistant (acting) editor of *Westminster Review*. Friendship with Herbert Spencer and George Henry Lewes, critic and author.
1854	Publishes translation of Feuerbach's *The Essence of Christianity*. Takes up residence in Germany with Lewes. Meets Liszt. Begins a translation of Spinoza's *Ethics*.
1855	Returns to England, where she and Lewes take up residence in Richmond. Evans is not received by her family.
1856	Begins to write fiction.
1858	*Scenes of Clerical Life* published under the name George Eliot. Dickens writes Eliot that he is sure she is a woman; her identity is made public after the book is attributed to a dissenting clergyman of Nuneaton.
1859	Publishes *Adam Bede*. Established as leading woman novelist of the day.
1860	*The Mill on the Floss*.
1861	*Silas Marner*. Begins writing *Romola*.
1862	Publishes *Romola* serially in *The Cornhill Magazine,* of which Lewes has recently become consulting editor.
1866	*Felix Holt, The Radical*.
1868	*The Spanish Gypsy*.
1869	Meets John Cross, a wealthy businessman.
1871–72	*Middlemarch* published in parts.
1874	*The Legend of Jubal and Other Poems*.
1876	Publication of *Daniel Deronda* in parts.
1877	Eliot and Lewes received by Princess Louise and the Crown Princess of Germany, daughters of Queen Victoria.
1878	Eliot and Lewes meet Turgenev, who refers to Eliot as the greatest living novelist. Lewes dies November 30 of cancer.
1879	Works on preparing edition of essays, *Impressions of Theophrastus Such,* for press. John Blackwood, her publisher, dies on October 29.
1880	Eliot marries John Cross (twenty years her junior). Dies on December 22 at her home in Cheyne Walk.
1885	John Cross publishes *George Eliot's Life*.

Contributors

HAROLD BLOOM, Sterling Professor of the Humanities at Yale University, is the author of *The Anxiety of Influence, Poetry and Repression,* and many other volumes of literary criticism. His forthcoming study, *Freud: Transference and Authority,* attempts a full-scale reading of all of Freud's major writings. A MacArthur Prize Fellow, he is general editor of five series of literary criticism published by Chelsea House. During 1987–88, he was appointed Charles Eliot Norton Professor of Poetry at Harvard University.

J. HILLIS MILLER is Distinguished Professor of English and Comparative Literature at the University of California, Irvine. Among his many books are *The Poetry of Reality* and *The Disappearance of God.* His latest book is *Ethics of Reading.*

BARBARA HARDY is Professor of English Literature at Birbeck College, University of London. Her books include critical studies of George Eliot and Jane Austen.

KATHLEEN BLAKE is Associate Professor of English at the University of Washington. She is the author of *Play, Games, and Sport: The Literary Works of Lewis Carroll.*

NEIL HERTZ is Professor in the Humanities Center at The Johns Hopkins University and is the author of *The End of the Line.*

JAN B. GORDON is Professor of English at Tokyo University of Foreign Studies. He has most recently published articles on Anne Brontë, Mark Twain, and on English poetry in polylingual Singapore.

ALEXANDER WELSH is Professor of English at the University of California, Los Angeles. His works include *The Hero of the Waverley Novels* and *George Eliot and Blackmail.*

PATRICIA MCKEE teaches English at Dartmouth College and is the author of *Heroic Commitment in Richardson, Eliot, and James.*

153

Bibliography

Adam, Ian, ed. *This Particular Web: Essays on* Middlemarch. Toronto: University of Toronto Press, 1975.

Adams, Harriet Farwell. "Dorothea and 'Miss Brooke' in *Middlemarch.*" *Nineteenth-Century Fiction* 39, no. 1 (June 1984): 69–90.

Allen, Walter. *George Eliot.* New York: Macmillan, 1964.

Ashton, Rosemary. *George Eliot.* Oxford: Oxford University Press, 1983.

Beaty, Jerome. "History by Indirection: The Era of Reform in *Middlemarch.*" *Victorian Studies* 1 (December 1957): 973–79.

———. Middlemarch *from Notebook to Novel: A Study of George Eliot's Creative Method.* Urbana: University of Illinois Press, 1960.

Bedient, Calvin. *Architects of the Self: George Eliot, D. H. Lawrence, and E. M. Forster.* Berkeley: University of California Press, 1972.

Beer, Patricia. *Reader, I Married Him: A Study of the Women Characters of Jane Austen, Charlotte Brontë, Elizabeth Gaskell and George Eliot.* New York: Barnes & Noble, 1974.

Bellringer, Alan W. "The Study of Provincial Life in *Middlemarch.*" *English* 28 (1979): 219–47.

Bennett, Joan. *George Eliot: Her Mind and Her Art.* Cambridge: Cambridge University Press, 1948.

Booth, Alison. "Little Dorrit and Dorothea Brooke: Interpreting the Heroines of History." *Nineteenth-Century Literature* 41, no. 2 (September 1986): 190–216.

Bonaparte, Felicia. *The Triptych and the Cross: The Central Myths of George Eliot's Poetic Imagination.* New York: New York University Press, 1979.

———. *Will and Destiny: Morality and Tragedy in George Eliot's Novels.* New York: New York University Press, 1975.

Buckley, Jerome H., ed. *The Worlds of Victorian Fiction.* Cambridge: Harvard University Press, 1975.

Carroll, David. "Unity through Analogy: An Intepretation of *Middlemarch.*" *Victorian Studies* 2 (June 1959): 305–16.

———, ed. *George Eliot: The Critical Heritage.* New York: Barnes & Noble, 1971.

Christ, Carol. "Aggression and Providential Death in George Eliot's Fiction." *Novel* 9 (1976): 130–40.

Creeger, George R., ed. *George Eliot: A Collection of Critical Essays.* Englewood Cliffs, N.J.: Prentice-Hall, 1970.

Daiches, David. *George Eliot: Middlemarch*. Great Neck, N.Y.: Barron's Educational Series, 1963.

Dentith, Simon. *George Eliot*. Sussex, England: Harvester, 1986.

Doyle, Mary Ellen. *The Sympathetic Response: George Eliot's Fictional Rhetoric*. London: Associated University Presses, 1981.

Edwards, Lee. "Women, Energy, and *Middlemarch*." *The Massachusetts Review* 13 (1972): 223–38.

Emery, Laura Comer. *George Eliot's Creative Conflict: The Other Side of Silence*. Berkeley: University of California Press, 1976.

Ermarth, Elizabeth Deeds. *George Eliot*. Twayne's English Author Series. Boston: Twayne, 1985.

———. *Realism and Consensus in the English Novel*. Princeton: Princeton University Press, 1983.

Garrett, Peter K. *The Victorian Multiplot Novel: Studies in Dialogical Form*. New Haven: Yale University Press, 1980.

Gilbert, Sandra M., and Susan Gubar. *The Madwoman in the Attic: The Woman Writer and the Nineteenth-Century Literary Imagination*. New Haven: Yale University Press, 1979.

Ginsburg, Michal Peled. "Pseudonym, Epigraphs, and Narrative Voice: *Middlemarch* and the Deceit of Authorship." *ELH* 47 (1980): 542–58.

Graver, Suzanne. *George Eliot and Community: A Study in Social Theory and Fictional Form*. Berkeley: University of California Press, 1984.

Greenberg, Robert A. "Plexuses and Ganglia: Scientific Allusion in *Middlemarch*." *Nineteenth-Century Fiction* 30 (1975): 33–52.

Hardy, Barbara, ed. *Critical Essays on George Eliot*. London: Routledge & Kegan Paul, 1970.

———. *Forms of Feeling in Victorian Fiction*. London: Peter Owen, 1985.

———. *The Novels of George Eliot: A Study in Form*. New York: Oxford University Press, 1967.

———. *Rituals and Feeling in the Novels of George Eliot*. Swansea, Wales: University College of Swansea, 1973.

———, ed. Middlemarch: *Critical Approaches to the Novel*. London: Athlone, 1967.

Harvey, W. J. *The Art of George Eliot*. New York: Oxford University Press, 1962.

Holloway, John. "Narrative Process in *Middlemarch*." In *Narrative and Structure: Exploratory Essays*. Cambridge: Cambridge University Press, 1979.

Hornback, Bert G. "The Organization of *Middlemarch*." *Papers on Language and Literature* 2 (1966): 169–75.

Hulme, Hilda M. "*Middlemarch* as Science Fiction: Notes on Language and Imagery." *Novel* 2 (1968): 36–45.

Isaacs, Neil D. "*Middlemarch*: Crescendo of Obligatory Drama." *Nineteenth-Century Fiction* 18 (1963): 21–34.

Kakar, H. S. *The Persistent Self: An Approach to* Middlemarch. Delhi: Doaba House, 1977.

Ker, I. T. "George Eliot's Rhetoric of Enthusiasm." *Essays in Criticism* 26 (1976): 134–55.

Kiely, Robert. "The Limits of Dialogue in *Middlemarch*." In *The Worlds of Victorian Fiction*, edited by Jerome H. Buckley. Harvard English Studies 6. Cambridge: Harvard University Press, 1975.

Knoepflmacher, U. C. "*Middlemarch:* Affirmation through Compromise." In *Laughter and Despair: Readings in Ten Novels of the Victorian Era.* Berkeley: University of California Press, 1971.

———. "*Middlemarch:* An Avuncular View." *Nineteenth-Century Fiction* 30 (1975): 53–81.

———. *Religious Humanism and the Victorian Novel: George Eliot, Walter Pater, and Samuel Butler.* Princeton: Princeton University Press, 1965.

Leavis, F. R. *The Great Tradition: George Eliot, Henry James, Joseph Conrad.* London: Chatto & Windus, 1962.

Levine, George. "Determinism and Responsibility in the Works of George Eliot." *PMLA* 77 (1962): 268–79.

———. "George Eliot's Hypothesis of Reality." *Nineteenth-Century Fiction* 35 (1980): 1–28.

———. "Repression and Vocation in George Eliot: A Review Essay." *Women and Literature* 2, no. 7 (1979): 3–13.

Lundberg, Patricia Lorimer. "George Eliot: Mary Ann Evans's Subversive Tool in *Middlemarch?*" *Studies in the Novel* 18, no. 3 (Fall 1986): 270–82.

McSweeney, Kerry. *Middlemarch.* Unwin Critical Library. London: Allen & Unwin, 1986.

Mann, Karen B. *The Language that Makes George Eliot's Fiction.* Baltimore: The Johns Hopkins University Press, 1983.

Marcus, Steven. "Literature and Social Theory: Starting in with George Eliot." In *Representations: Essays on Literature and Society.* New York: Random House, 1975.

Mason, Michael York. "*Middlemarch* and Science: Problems of Life and Mind." *The Review of English Studies* 22 (1971): 151–69.

Meckier, Jerome. "'That Arduous Invention': *Middlemarch* Versus the Modern Satirical Novel." *Ariel* 4, no. 9 (1978): 31–63.

Mintz, Alan. *George Eliot and the Novel of Vocation.* Cambridge: Harvard University Press, 1978.

Myers, William. *The Teaching of George Eliot.* Totowa, N.J.: Barnes & Noble, 1984.

Newton, K. M. *George Eliot, Romantic Humanist: A Study of the Philosophical Structure of Her Novels.* Totowa, N.J.: Barnes & Noble, 1981.

Oldfield, Derek. "The Language of the Novel, the Character of Dorothea." In Middlemarch: *Critical Approaches,* edited by Barbara Hardy. New York: Oxford University Press, 1967.

Pinion, F. B. *A George Eliot Companion: Literary Achievement and Modern Significance.* Totowa, N.J.: Barnes & Noble, 1981.

Redinger, Ruby V. *George Eliot: The Emergent Self.* New York: Knopf, 1975.

Ringler, Ellen. "*Middlemarch:* A Feminist Perspective." *Studies in the Novel* 15 (Spring 1983): 55–60.

Roberts, Neil. *George Eliot: Her Beliefs and Her Art.* Pittsburgh: University of Pittsburgh Press, 1975.

Scott, James F. "George Eliot, Positivism, and the Social Vision of *Middlemarch.*" *Victorian Studies* 16 (1972): 59–76.

Shuttleworth, Sally. *George Eliot and Nineteenth-Century Science.* Cambridge: Cambridge University Press, 1984.

Smith, Jane S. "The Reader as Part of the Fiction: *Middlemarch.*" *Texas Studies in Literature and Language* 19 (1977): 188–203.

Stump, Reva. *Movement and Vision in George Eliot's Novels.* Seattle: University of Washington Press, 1959.

Stwertka, Eve Marie. "The Web of Utterance: *Middlemarch.*" *Texas Studies in Literature and Language* 19 (1977): 179–87.

Swann, Brian. "*Middlemarch* and Myth." *Nineteenth-Century Fiction* 28 (1973): 210–14.

————. "*Middlemarch:* Realism and Symbolic Form." *ELH* 39 (1972): 279–308.

Van Ghent, Dorothy. *The English Novel: Form and Function.* New York: Rinehart, 1953.

Weisenfarth, Joseph. *George Eliot's Mythmaking.* Heidelberg: Carl Winter, Universitatsverlag, 1977.

————. "*Middlemarch:* The Language of Art." *PMLA* 97 (1982): 363–77.

Witemeyer, Hugh. *George Eliot and the Visual Arts.* New Haven: Yale University Press, 1979.

Wright, T. R. "*Middlemarch* as a Religious Novel, or Life without God." In *Images of Belief in Literature,* edited by David Jasper. New York: St. Martin's, 1984.

Acknowledgments

"Optic and Semiotic in *Middlemarch*" by J. Hillis Miller from *The Worlds of Victorian Fiction* (Harvard English Studies 6), edited by Jerome H. Buckley, © 1975 by the President and Fellows of Harvard College. Reprinted by permission of Harvard University, Department of English and American Literature and Language.

"Middlemarch: Public and Private Worlds" by Barbara Hardy from *Particularities: Readings in George Eliot* by Barbara Hardy, © 1982 by Barbara Hardy. Reprinted by permission.

"*Middlemarch* and the Woman Question" by Kathleen Blake from *Nineteenth-Century Fiction* 31, no. 3 (December 1976), © 1976 by the Regents of the University of California. Reprinted by permission of the University of California Press.

"Recognizing Casaubon" by Neil Hertz from *Glyph Textual Studies* 6, edited by Rodolphe Gasché, Carol Jacobs, and Henry Sussman, © 1979 by The Johns Hopkins University Press, Baltimore/London. Reprinted by permission of The Johns Hopkins University Press.

"Origins, *Middlemarch,* Endings: George Eliot's Crisis of the Antecedent" by Jan B. Gordon from *George Eliot: Centenary Essays and an Unpublished Fragment,* edited by Anne Smith, © 1980 by Vision Press Ltd. Reprinted by permission of Vision Press Ltd., and Barnes and Noble Books, Totowa, New Jersey.

"Knowledge in *Middlemarch*" by Alexander Welsh from *George Eliot and Blackmail* by Alexander Welsh, © 1985 by the President and Fellows of Harvard College. Reprinted by permission of Harvard University Press.

"Power as Partiality in *Middlemarch*" by Patricia McKee from *Heroic Commitment in Richardson, Eliot, and James* by Patricia McKee, © 1986 by Princeton University Press. Reprinted by permission of Princeton University Press.

Index